I0419046

THE
DIGITAL
HUMAN
ADVANTAGE

Also by Asha Saxena

The AI Factor

THE DIGITAL HUMAN ADVANTAGE

DRIVING BUSINESS GROWTH THROUGH INTELLIGENT DIGITAL AGENTS

ASHA SAXENA

A POST HILL PRESS BOOK

The Digital Human Advantage:
Driving Business Growth Through Intelligent Digital Agents

ISBN: 979-8-89565-161-2
ISBN (eBook): 979-8-89565-162-9

Cover design by Conroy Accord
Interior design and composition by Greg Johnson, Textbook Perfect

This book, as well as any other Post Hill Press publications, may be purchased in bulk quantities at a special discounted rate. Contact orders@posthillpress.com for more information.

Post Hill Press
New York • Nashville
posthillpress.com

Published in the United States of America
1 2 3 4 5 6 7 8 9 10

This book is dedicated to my parents—
my mom, Raj Khanna, and my dad, Bhim Sen Khanna—
who I miss so dearly every single day.
My mom's dedication, discipline, hard work, and resilience,
and my father's patience and quiet strength
have profoundly shaped my journey and who I am.

And to my husband, Rajeev Saxena,
whose unwavering support and partnership center me.

And to Siddharth and Veronika Saxena,
and Milan and Shaleen Saxena—
you are my greatest joy, my constant inspiration,
and my deepest pride.

Contents

Foreword

In the tapestry of technological evolution, few threads have been woven with as much anticipation and trepidation as artificial intelligence. As we stand at this pivotal moment in history, where the digital and human realms increasingly converge, Asha Saxena's *The Digital Human Advantage* arrives as both lighthouse and compass.

I first met Asha through our shared interest in how technology transforms business and society. Her ability to navigate the complex intersection of data science, leadership, and human values immediately struck me. What distinguishes Asha in the crowded field of technology thought leaders is her insistence that technological advancement must be guided by ethical principles and human-centered design; this book exemplifies that philosophy.

As the Director of the Institute for Data Science at New Jersey Institute of Technology (NJIT), I've witnessed firsthand the dramatic acceleration of AI capabilities. The emergence of digital humans—AI-enabled entities that simulate human appearance, voice, and behavior—represents perhaps the most profound development in this evolution. These entities stand at the frontier of what's possible, promising to reshape our workplaces, services, and daily interactions in ways both thrilling and challenging.

The urgency of understanding this technology cannot be overstated. We find ourselves at a historical inflection point where digital humans are rapidly advancing from rudimentary prototypes to increasingly sophisticated agents capable of complex interactions. Many organizations are already deploying these technologies, often without fully understanding their implications or potential. This knowledge gap creates both risk and missed opportunity.

What makes *The Digital Human Advantage* essential reading is its comprehensive yet accessible approach to this complex subject. Asha doesn't merely catalog the technical capabilities of digital humans, she explores their developmental journey from pre-conscious entities to potential sage-like advisors. This framework provides a nuanced understanding of where we are and where we might be headed.

The book's greatest strength lies in its balanced perspective. Asha acknowledges both sides of the digital human debate—those who fear job displacement, privacy erosion, and manipulation, alongside those who envision unprecedented productivity gains and creative possibilities. Yet she moves us beyond this binary thinking toward a more sophisticated understanding: digital humans mirror both our strengths and our flaws. They are, in essence, reflections of ourselves.

This insight leads to perhaps the most crucial lesson of the book: the success of digital humans depends not just on sophisticated algorithms and vast datasets, but on ethical leadership and clear principles. As Asha eloquently puts it, "Along with the mountains of data we feed them, we must also lead by example, with the principles and behavior we expect of each other." This recognition—that we bear responsibility for what we create—transforms the conversation from purely technical to deeply human.

For executives navigating this rapidly evolving landscape, *The Digital Human Advantage* offers more than conceptual understanding. The book provides a structured methodology for implementing digital humans responsibly across various business contexts. From designing appropriate personas to establishing governance frameworks, Asha offers practical guidance informed by years of experience in data leadership.

The timing of this work is particularly meaningful. We stand at the threshold of what may be the most significant technological transition since the advent of the internet—the widespread integration of artificial intelligence into nearly every aspect of business and society. Organizations that thoughtfully incorporate digital humans will likely gain substantial competitive advantages in terms of efficiency, customer experience, and innovation. Those that ignore the trend or implement it poorly may find themselves struggling to remain relevant.

What particularly resonates with my own research in high-performance computing and data science is Asha's emphasis on the complementary relationship between human and artificial intelligence. Rather than replacing human creativity and judgment, properly designed digital humans can enhance our capabilities by handling routine tasks and providing insights that might otherwise remain hidden in vast seas of data. This synergistic approach creates space for humans to focus on what we do best: imagine, empathize, and innovate.

The framework presented in this book aligns with what I've observed in successful AI implementations: technology must serve clear business objectives while adhering to ethical principles and robust governance. Asha's methodology provides a roadmap for achieving this balance, ensuring that digital humans serve as beneficial partners rather than problematic liabilities.

For leaders preparing their organizations for this future, *The Digital Human Advantage* serves as both strategic guide and practical manual. It addresses not only the capabilities of digital humans but also their appropriate application across industries and contexts. Most importantly, it never loses sight of the human element at the center of this technological revolution.

As we navigate the coming decade, the principles outlined in these pages will become increasingly relevant. The digital transformation of business and society continues to accelerate, with AI as its driving force. Organizations that understand how to leverage digital humans effectively—with appropriate governance, clear purpose, and ethical boundaries—will be positioned to thrive.

I encourage you to approach this book with both optimism and critical thinking. The potential benefits of digital humans are immense, but realizing them requires thoughtful implementation and ongoing vigilance. Asha provides the framework for this balanced approach, drawing on her extensive experience and conversations with leading experts in the field.

The Digital Human Advantage arrives at precisely the moment we need it most—when possibility and responsibility must advance hand in hand. I am confident that this book will serve as an essential resource for leaders seeking to navigate the exciting yet challenging frontier of human-AI collaboration.

David A. Bader, PhD
Distinguished Professor
Director, Institute for Data Science
New Jersey Institute of Technology

Dr. David A. Bader is a leading figure in high-performance computing and data science. He is widely known for his groundbreaking work in parallel algorithms, supercomputing architecture, and real-world analytics applications. Coauthor of over three hundred scholarly papers, he was also the principal figure in the creation of the world's first Linux-based supercomputer in 1998. Dr. Bader was inducted into the University of Maryland's Innovation Hall of Fame in 2022, and into the Mimms Museum of Technology and Art's (formerly the Computer Museum of America) Hall of Fame in 2025.

Introduction

Many people are nervous, even afraid of digital human agents, those voices on our phones or those responsive, humanlike images on our screens: "Can I trust them not to deceive me?" "Will they take away my privacy?" "Will they take over my job, my company, or my country?"

Others are all in: "Digital humans are my friends, my assistants, my companions." "They listen to my problems." "They make my life easy." "They give me time to be more creative." "They'll make the world a better place."

Both sides have a point, but neither side is asking all the right questions or giving complete answers. Yes, digital humans are incredibly powerful tools. They are a profound inflection point in our technology journey. They can use artificial intelligence and digital simulations of our appearance and voice to do things that seem like magic. But what we miss is the fact that *digital humans mirror both the strengths* **and** *the flaws of humanity*. Like Microsoft's infamous chatbot, Tay,[1] digital humans can quickly absorb and amplify the negative aspects of human interaction. That is, unless they are guided by ethical leadership and empathy.

AI-enabled digital humans are a reflection of <u>us</u>.
They mirror both our strengths and our flaws.

An AI system's business objectives are supremely important, as this book will demonstrate, but they are not enough. To ensure their long-term success as well as ours, we must remember that *digital human agents are a reflection of* ***us***. The real issue is that, along with the mountains of data we feed them, we must also *lead by example*, with the principles and behavior we expect of each other.

This book will explore the possible advantages that digital humans represent and offer a methodology for realizing them. But it will also present a framework for doing so responsibly. In the end, whether these agents ever become "alive" or not, what we teach them at every stage of their existence, will make all the difference.

AI systems in general have ***a five-stage pattern of development*** (or evolution, if you prefer). This is a pattern that can make them better partners—that is ***if*** we guide them well at each stage:

The first is that of ***a preconscious being***, driven only by basic stimuli. Like a well-trained animal, it can quickly respond to input and even do things repeatedly in a way that make it seem rational. But for systems like these, without the use of AI, there is no true, contextual awareness involved. You could think of the key trait as blind but trainable ***obedience***. Sometimes, it *seems* like such systems are being willful, especially when they disregard our wishes. At this stage, however, what seems like stubborn obstinance from a computerized system is really just flawed or incomplete input. The developer's role here is not to assign the system a personality but to be clear and concise about the data being used for the AI model and the instructions for processing it.

The second stage is that of ***a learner***. Just as a curious child explores a new environment, more advanced AI systems recognize input patterns and adapt to new data using machine learning.

They learn entirely from the data they receive; they start in a *blank slate*, without innate ideas of their own. Their key trait here might be described as ***curiosity***. The developer's role here is obvious. Not only must the data be vetted for bias and other defects, the AI's output also must be monitored. A digital human at this stage is capable of both supervised and unsupervised learning, but both the AI's objectives and its results are our responsibility.

The third stage, that of ***a synthesizer***, is where many digital human agents are today. By integrating advanced natural language programming, symbolic reasoning, and complex decision-making models, such an entity can closely imitate human behavior and respond naturally to real time input. Although they are still not self-aware (we believe), their key trait is best described as ***reflection***. They can envision vast amounts of data, in context, and draw conclusions as to its broader meaning. This is arguably the greatest challenge for digital human developers: Not only must the datasets be robust and well governed, the system must also adhere to principles of transparency, non-maleficence, and respect for human rights and autonomy.

The fourth stage, that of ***a companion***, is difficult enough for humans, much less for the digital counterparts we create. Digital human companions today are only just beginning to simulate contextual awareness, empathy modeling, and ethical reasoning. This has produced remarkable early results, due in part due to AI's ability to create personalized interactions, and to the emergence of affective computing.* An attribute of this might be described as ***compassion***. However, it will take time and a lot of work and supervision before we can put any of our digital humans on par

* Affective computing emerged in the mid-1990s as a multidisciplinary field for developing systems capable of recognizing, interpreting, and simulating human emotions. MIT professor Rosalind Picard defines it as "computing that relates to, arises from, or deliberately influences emotions."

with Confucius's definition of a "virtuous person"—someone who lives in harmony with others.

The final stage, that of ***a sage***, is perhaps something we can only hope for in a digital human agent. But if it happens, it will be in the future, well after ***artificial general intelligence*** (or AGI) becomes a practical reality. We may be fortunate enough to work with digital humans who possess the AI equivalent of ***wisdom***. But to have such autonomous, beneficial partners and cocreators in our future, we must do everything in our power to lead by example *now*.

•———•

This book is divided into two parts. In PART ONE, Chapter 1 presents the foundational ideas, concepts, and broad examples of what digital humans are like today, what they can become, and their potential to transform our lives. Chapter 2 is an exploration of core technologies like machine learning, deep learning, natural language processing, and real-time audio and video rendering—all of which make digital humans able to interact with us with ever-increasing realism. It also looks at how Web3 and related technology will affect the bigger picture.

Chapter 3 is a detailed discussion of ***the digital human advantage***, and how these emerging entities can increase our productivity across multiple industries and environments. This is followed in Chapter 4 by a look at the digital human ecosystem of digital assistants, collaborators, companions, twins, and the fifth "species"—us—and how they can work well with one another.

The final chapter in PART ONE (Chapter 5) covers the ethical and societal implications of creating and using digital human agents. Far from being a "nice to have" feature, developers must have a framework that can counter emotional manipulation, misinformation, bias, and privacy abuse. The chapter also tackles the thorny issue of job displacement.

PART TWO begins with a general operating model for digital human agents. In my previous book, *The AI Factor*, I presented a basic business and data framework for implementing artificial intelligence projects.* Based on this framework, Chapter 6 will lay out several of the likely business objectives involved in deploying digital humans in different types of businesses. It will also spell out the requirements in terms of data readiness, capabilities, data literacy, and governance.

Chapters 7 and 8 will deal with the practical details, beginning with the different personas a digital human can embody and the impact on real-world situations. This is followed by a methodology for digital human design and development—from discovery, through testing and evaluation. This also includes stakeholder engagement and ethics audits.

Chapter 9 is a compilation of industry experts' experience and opinions in their work with AI and digital human agents—and their invaluable advice on best practices. Chapter 10 outlines the current state of the technology, strategic recommendations for the immediate future, and some informed predictions on the long-term societal impacts and the evolving role of digital humans in advanced AI and robotics.

In researching this book, I was fortunate to speak with other experts in AI and digital agency, many of whom are friends and colleagues. They affirmed many of the principles I've outlined here. The potential benefits of well-designed digital human

* In brief, this includes determining the *type* of business involved, based on growth potential and risk tolerance, and the company's *data readiness*—its facility with and access to high-quality data.

agents outweigh the risks. Without dissent, they testified to its significance in terms of increased productivity, efficiency, and innovation. They also affirmed my deepest conviction that the risks of digital humans, while real, can be handled if we carefully consider their ethical, societal, and organizational implications.

The whole point of creating autonomous, AI-enabled digital humans is to relieve us of the *burden* of tedious, routine, and repetitive decisions. However, it does not relieve us of the *responsibility* for those decisions. It is my hope that this book will help you accomplish both ideals.

Unlike us, digital humans can *actually* multitask. They can analyze information and make multiple, routine decisions simultaneously, at lightning speed—limited only by processing capacity and the quality of their data. They also do not require sleep or overtime pay. Properly designed, they can also learn how to make routine decisions without our constant input or supervision. If we teach them well, those decisions will align with our values and principles. In the end they will end up freeing us busy humans—giving us back the time to imagine new possibilities and make better decisions.

PART ONE

FOUNDATIONS AND CONCEPTS

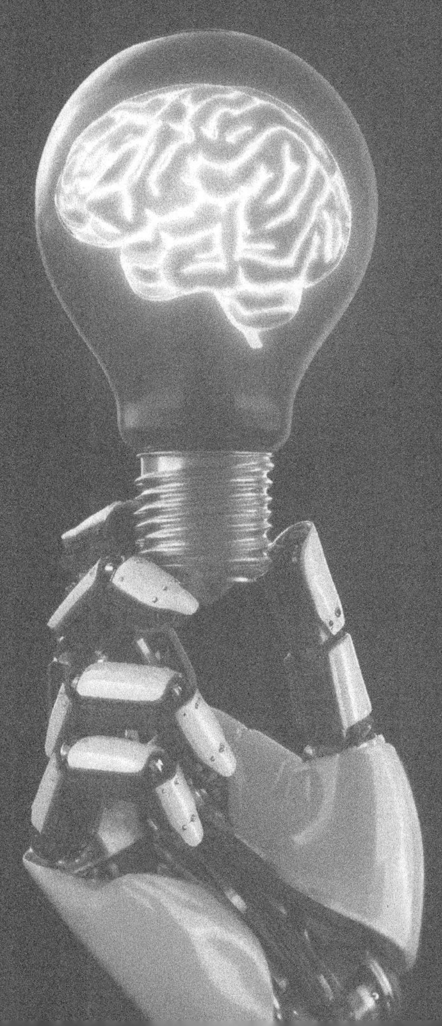

CHAPTER 1

Introducing Digital Humans

It's 6 A.M. Pam, a busy young CEO, has already begun her morning routine when she gets a video call from her favorite assistant, Izzy. Calmly and with a touch of humor, Izzy informs her of an emergency teleconference that needs to happen right away. Several investors are getting worried about the product launch, and they want to review the supply chain and delivery details.

At Pam's request, Izzy clears a one-hour window, diplomatically rescheduling other meetings and inviting the worried investors (and the COO, whose schedule she also rearranged to fit that meeting in) to a brief teleconference. She also creates a summary of the relevant data and a simple, five-slide presentation.

The cabs in New York are unusually tied up that morning, so Izzy arranges to send a company car—a hybrid, of course. With a smile, Izzy wishes Pam a great day and makes sure that Pam's coffee order will be there when she arrives.

Pam's dream assistant is not a human being: she is a digital human agent.

The interactions of Pam and Izzy are fictitious, but the scene is not a fantasy. This story is a vivid preview of the very near future of business, where digital humans—AI-enabled virtual entities—increasingly become part of our lives. As this book will illustrate, they are already assuming roles traditionally held by humans. These roles are typically *supportive* in nature. They can be customer service agents, personal advisors, collaborative teammates, and even empathetic companions. In the not too distant future, they may even act as digital stand-ins for human personnel, providing continuity for employees who are absent temporarily—or when their presence is needed in multiple locations simultaneously.

Digital human agents are a branch of high performance computing that merges artificial intelligence, machine learning, and other, present-day technologies with intricate human behavior models. As we will see, the results are interactions that humans find not only practical and efficient but also feel are real and engaging.

Digital humans go beyond the capabilities of standard chatbots: They are not simplistic, animated figures bound by rigid scripts, nor are they *passive interfaces*, waiting for explicit instructions. Rather, digital humans act as proactive partners, anticipating our needs and initiating certain actions independently.

This isn't magic. As we'll explore in the next chapter, digital humans are founded in very real science. Current technologies enable them to process and learn from data in real time (artificial intelligence and machine leaning) as well as interact with their human counterparts' speech, appearance, and even emotional cues (natural language processing, computer vision, and emotion AI). Advanced, real-time 3D modeling and speech synthesis technologies also create a humanlike appearance—one that is able to respond appropriately, and even nonverbally to the user.

In the foreseeable future, digital humans will do more than simply alleviate mundane tasks, they will enhance our capacity for creativity and innovation. By handling routine matters efficiently, digital human agents will free humans to explore greater possibilities, brainstorm more innovative solutions, and imagine the strategies that will shape our future.

The 24-7 Service Revolution

Digital human agents have many potential roles, as we will explore throughout this book. As the technology proves itself in everyday life and business, it is likely that most of us will work with these digital companions on a daily basis. However, for business leaders concerned primarily with customer service costs and efficiency, digital humans represent an immediate and revolutionary change. They offer the potential to provide consistent, high-quality, and personalized service at any time—without the traditional constraints of human staffing.

Digital humans have certain advantages over their natural human counterparts. Consider this scenario:

The Never-Tired Concierge

Traditional luxury hotels pride themselves on bespoke concierge service. Even mid-range hotels are acutely aware of the need to proactively serve their guests' needs. But even the most dedicated human concierge team has its limitations. Digital concierges can:

- **Provide instant service to multiple guests, simultaneously, and anywhere there is a screen or device—even the guest's smartphone**
- **Speak in many languages without missing important cultural nuances**

- **Perfectly remember every guest's preference and make the right recommendations**
- **Offer the same level of cheerful, patient service—at 4 p.m. or 4 a.m.**

When properly planned, and when using the right data responsibly, there is no question that such a digital human can add to the bottom line. Better still, such an agent can also be a bridge to actual human staff. When a guest's issues are unexpected or fall outside normal parameters, a digital concierge can easily reach out to its human counterpart.

A number of hotel chains implementing digital concierges have reported significant increases in guest satisfaction scores for after-hours requests, as well as notable reductions in staffing costs. Using advanced natural language processing (**NLP**) algorithms, computer vision technology, and emotional AI, these agents create responsive interactions that mimic human conversation patterns. Unlike traditional digital interfaces that guests merely use, digital humans create experiences that they remember. Other customer-facing businesses have had similar results.

The Financial Advisor Who Knows You

Financial institutions have long struggled with balancing personalized service and operational efficiency. Digital humans are changing this equation:

- **They recognize returning customers and can recall their financial profiles and investment history**
- **They can explain complex products without the pressure of a sales commission**
- **They can provide consistent information while adapting the explanation to each customer's financial literacy level**
- **They can offer judgment-free assistance for sensitive financial situations**

Banks and investment firms implementing digital humans in this way could free their human advisors to focus on more complex financial planning activities. This in turn could increase customer satisfaction and high-value product adoption. Obviously, however, a digital human interface for a financial institution, just like any other trusted, confidential entity, would be subject to strict privacy and fiduciary requirements.

The Larger Business Case

When discussing digital human agents, it's reasonable to ask some questions:

- "Isn't this just some flashy new technology looking for a problem?"
- "Are digital humans only about cutting staff?"
- "What genuine business value do they offer—for ***my*** business?"

To answer these questions, one must first consider what type of business is involved. What are the underlying business drivers that would be best served by deploying digital human agents?

Digital humans not only increase efficiency and reduce the cost of doing business, they also improve business processes, provide more time for creative innovation, and free humans to invent new business models.

In *The AI Factor*,[1] companies considering the business benefits of artificial intelligence were categorized by their inherent growth potential and by how willing its leaders are to innovate and take risks. The same analysis applies when considering AI-enabled digital humans. This will be covered in greater detail in Chapter 6, but a brief summary is warranted here:

- ***Optimizer* Organizations** (lower growth potential but less willing to innovate and take risks) would use digital humans to cut costs, increase efficiency, and improve existing processes.
- ***Extender* Organizations** (higher growth potential but less willing to innovate and take risks) would use digital humans to help increase business through more efficient initiative in marketing, sales, and mergers and acquisitions (M&A).
- ***Innovator* Organizations** (lower initial growth but greater willingness to innovate and take risks) would use them to accelerate team efficiency for research and new product development.
- ***Multiplier* Organizations** (higher growth potential *and* greater willingness to innovate and take risks) would use digital humans in multiple, well-coordinated teams in order to more effectively disrupt old business models and invent new ones.

For organizations focused mainly on improving efficiency (***Optimizers***), digital humans are an obvious win. For example, while ordinary chatbots can handle a large percentage of routine customer questions, they have disadvantages when it comes to complex or nuanced situations. According to one survey,[2] most consumers (86 percent) prefer to interact with a human agent, while many (71 percent) say they would be less likely to use a brand if it didn't have human customer service representatives available. Clearly, a digital human agent, able to sense human expression and respond in real time, will bridge that gap.

Once attuned to the needs of a company's customer base, digital human agents can be scaled across the enterprise, serving thousands of customers with the same level of quality—without incurring onerous staffing costs. Properly used, they solve a seemingly impossible business challenge: providing personalized, human-feeling service—at scale and around the clock—while also controlling costs.

Both ***Optimizers*** and ***Extenders*** can benefit from using digital humans in other ways. As customer service agents, they are ideally suited to collecting real-time customer intelligence, measuring both success rates and sentiment analyses, which can be used to improve internal processes and win new business.

Of course, digital human agents can do more than reduce staffing costs. As we'll explore later, they also can help improve a wide range of business activities, freeing their human counterparts to invent new ways of doing business. Their greatest impact may be their effects on teams—making them more capable and multiplying their companies' success.

The Great Interface Transformation

Throughout history, companies that recognized technology shifts early became great. Other organizations fell behind, especially if they dragged their feet or just followed the change blindly. This trend is especially true when it comes to bridging the gap between our data and technology tools and the people who need to use them.

Since the invention of digital technology, the volume and complexity of our data has grown exponentially. It is more and more difficult for decision-makers to understand data and make good decisions from it. Thankfully, the user interface between computers and humans has evolved remarkably over the years, giving humans a fighting chance to use all that data to their advantage. But not everyone takes advantage of this. Truly great organizations—companies that *thrive*—do not merely implement these interfaces: They transform them into mechanisms for competitive advantage.

In the 1940s through the very early 1980s, computing power was accessible only to data specialists. These were the technicians who had mastered the mysteries of the command line interface. Exceptional leaders and their companies recognized this limitation earlier than most. Beginning in the 1980s, Apple and others introduced new ***graphical user interfaces*** (or GUIs), giving ordinary people access to data. Technology was no longer just for technologists.

But GUIs alone were not enough to bridge the gap. Digital systems were still limited to passively responding to user actions and queries. People wondered if a digital interface could *proactively* engage with humans. In the 1990s, Microsoft tried to answer this question with Clippy, a crude, anthropomorphic assistant. Its cartoonish, often annoying nature was widely ridiculed.[3] It lacked the power of AI required to make it an effective digital assistant. But it also fueled the hope that digital systems could someday become proactive team members.

An answer to this problem emerged in the 2010s, when three technological "flywheels" reached critical velocity simultaneously. First, the raw processing power of cloud computing provided organizations with unprecedented computational resources. Second, the sheer volume, variety, and accessibility of data (collectively known as "big data") created the training environment for advanced machine learning and predictive artificial intelligence. Finally, vast neural networks allowed for the development of large language models (LLMs), enabling advanced text and voice recognition and predictive responses.

What if a computer interface was not just something you used, but someone with whom you collaborated?

The interface advances that emerged from this confluence included voice assistants like Apple's Siri and Amazon's Alexa. They also included many AI-powered chatbots for websites, mobile apps, and internet-enabled devices. These not only supplemented or replaced traditional help systems and call centers, they also challenged a basic premise of human-computer interaction: What if an interface was not something you just used, but someone with whom you collaborated?

The final phase (so far) in this interface evolution emerged around 2017, with what we now recognize as the digital human. In 2018, Google demonstrated Duplex, an AI system capable of making phone calls that sounded natural enough to pass as human. The release of ChatGPT and similar LLM platforms in late 2023 also demonstrated a near-human simulation of text comprehension and response. But most of all, these AI-based technologies were soon combined with 3D modeling and rendering techniques, making it possible to replicate human facial expressions and simulate real-world lighting, color, and texture effects.

Some companies have hesitated to adopt this shift—just as they and others have hesitated to adopt chatbots and AI in general. But great companies recognized this shift and have begun to apply it broadly to accelerate every aspect of their businesses. As this book will explore, the technology itself is not perfect, nor are its ethical implications. But the idea of our technology as a trusted agent or partner has finally arrived.

The Emotional Connection

What sets digital humans apart from chatbots is their ability to simulate emotional engagement with increasing accuracy. They can do this thanks to the emerging field known as Emotion AI,[4] the integration of emotional intelligence into artificial intelligence systems: They can make eye contact during an interaction, they can smile when you're pleased and express concern when you're troubled, and they remember your preferences and adapt to your communication style. This emotional intelligence is powered by sentiment analysis algorithms. These analyze facial expressions, voice modulation, and linguistic patterns to detect emotional states.[5] This enables a digital human agent to respond appropriately, bringing a human touch to digital interactions. As digital humans become more adept at imitating and mirroring human behavior, they will be seen increasingly as essential work companions.

It's true that our experience with some digital human agents still suffers from the "uncanny valley" experience, where the persona is close to that of a human but just different enough to make the human uncomfortable.[6] This problem will diminish over time as the technology matures. Even now, however, when organizations *transparently* communicate the artificial nature of their digital humans, while also delivering meaningful emotional connections, users report higher satisfaction rates, and willingness to continue engagement, compared to users interacting with standard AI systems.[7]

There are substantial business implications for using emotionally intelligent digital humans in multiple sectors. In customer service, for example, digital humans that recognize and appropriately respond to customer frustration can de-escalate tensions and improve resolution rates. Healthcare applications are especially promising. Emotionally responsive digital human agents tend to improve medication adherence and patient education outcomes.

Overall, companies implementing emotionally intelligent digital humans in a responsible manner, with access to the right data, can expect significant increases in customer and employee retention, not to mention overall productivity and innovation. All indications suggest that emotional connection will be a defining feature of tomorrow's business technology.

Group Dynamics and Agency

To understand the value of a work companion—digital or otherwise—it's important to realize how we all work better together in teams than we do as lone individuals. ***Human beings are social creatures by nature***; it's how we survived as a species. We do better when we're part of a mutually supportive group than when we're alone, even though we take that for granted at times.

The science is clear. In one study, research showed that groups of three to five people perform better at solving letters-to-numbers problems than even the best individuals.[8] In another study of 1,200 individuals, researchers found that "[...]interacting groups are as fast as the fastest individual and more efficient than the most efficient individual for complex tasks[...]."[9] Another study found, to no one's surprise, "[...]that teamwork has a significant positive effect on job satisfaction."[10]

The trouble is that positive group dynamics can be next to impossible without the help of team members who, although often working unseen or unnoticed, keep the wheels turning.

Countless books have been written about those who *lead* these groups of interconnected human beings; less attention is paid to those behind-the-scenes heroes who make things run smoothly—the agents who serve the interests of the team. Think of a human team member who's great at research, or one who can master a complex event schedule, or one who is prepared for a crisis even before it happens. Sometimes the word "assistant" is in their job description, but often it's just in their nature. They know how to keep things moving smoothly. Individuals like these—preferably more than just one lone, beleaguered assistant or intern—are integral to the success of any group.

The word "agent" has shades of meaning. It can mean someone who acts on behalf of another person or group, such as a financial or talent manager, an attorney, or even a member of Congress. It also means someone who is trusted to act *independently*, someone authorized to make choices, based on available information and resources, without being told what to do at each step. They are ultimately accountable for those choices, but their role is to do the things that their principal—an individual or a group—cannot easily do for themselves.

An agent is one who can be trusted to act independently (and accountably), to do those things that other team members cannot easily do themselves.

In an ideal world, everyone in a group is taking on the role of agent. From the head of an organization to the newest intern, each person should be acting in the best interests of the entire group—trusted by others to act independently in order to accomplish their objectives. But there's a big problem with that idea (other than our human flaws, that is): Agency through humans alone is not enough to meet all the challenges of today's world. There are too many variables, too much complexity, and too much information for groups of ordinary people to handle effectively. Just adding more and more members to the group often leads to costly, bureaucratic overload. Productivity technology, by itself, can actually magnify the problem—creating more and more data that requires decisions by human agents.

The answer, of course, is to recruit that very technology to become agents—serving the group's objectives with just the right balance of autonomy and accountability to the group. Rather than something to be feared, a digital human agent would instead be a welcome relief to teams struggling to cope with the demands of our data-intensive workplace.

Taking the First Steps

The journey toward implementing digital humans doesn't require a massive organizational overhaul. As later chapters will detail, most businesses can begin with focused use cases:

- Identify the type of business you are in, based on your potential for growth and your risk tolerance.
- Identify your biggest unsolved problems, the nature and quality of your data, and the solutions that represent the highest potential value.
- In the beginning, look for high-volume, routine interactions where people would benefit most from immediate, relevant, and emotionally intelligent responses.
- Always start with a digital human handling a specific domain of knowledge, built on a foundation of pretrained models, and fine-tuned with domain-specific data.
- Periodically analyze the interactions with digital humans. Continuously improve their responses and capabilities through reinforcement learning from human feedback.
- Gradually expand the digital human's role as customers and team members embrace the technology.

Successful implementations always view digital humans not as replacements for human employees, but as partners. They can handle routine matters, allowing your human team to focus on complex, high-value interactions. Over time, and as such systems earn our trust, digital human agents will continue to evolve from specialized tools to valued, indispensable members of your team.

The question is not whether digital humans will transform business at every level imaginable—the question is whether you will be leading this transformation or trying to catch up with those who embraced it first.

The age of digital humans is already here. Are you ready to join it?

CHAPTER 2

Technological Foundations

Think about the last time you interacted with a lifelike digital character. Perhaps it was the soothing, no-nonsense voice of Siri or Alexa. Or maybe it was something more visual, like a fellow player (or a simulated character) in a video game. It could also be an animated customer service rep or a virtual assistant. Whatever the experience, what made it feel authentic? What made you uncomfortable? Did the experience help you do something more easily or just make it harder?

If your experience was a poor one, the chances are that it was due to limits in technology. The uncanny valley feeling you get when dealing with an almost human replica means that it lacks the means to read our body language and respond to it authentically. When such a character is frustratingly unhelpful, it means it's relying on a narrow, scripted dataset, not responding in real time or learning from the interaction. But all that is about to change.

Exponential advances in processing power, bandwidth, and access to big data have made existing technologies—working in tandem—capable of having complex, humanlike interactions.

It's true that digital humans are the product of many *existing* technologies. Some, like AI and machine learning (ML), have been around for decades; others, like 3D animation, are in the CGI characters we see in movies and video games today. But ***all of them were constrained by the limits of technology***—limits on processing power, on network bandwidth, and on access to data.

That is, until now: Exponential advances in these core technologies have made truly helpful digital humans possible. Working in tandem, these technologies are now becoming capable of having complex, humanlike interactions with us.

To better understand the technologies involved in creating a digital human, this chapter will use the metaphors of brain, soul, and body. I know it's tempting to think of these things literally, especially the "soul" part. But as long as you remember that digital humans are simply advanced tools, without human will or consciousness, these metaphors will serve as a useful framework.

The Brain of a Digital Human

The "brain" of a digital human is a combination of data technologies that serve as its ability to mimic human thinking and problem-solving. Some may think of this as consciousness or self-awareness, but that would be a mistake: These technologies are simply a very fast way to predict outcomes and make decisions, based on available data and the ability to learn from new data, all in real time.

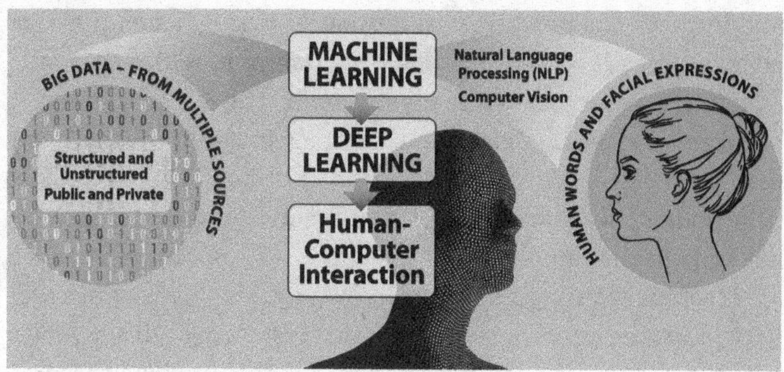

The AI components of a digital human's "brain."

Artificial intelligence (**AI**), the general data science that makes all this possible, is the broad field whereby high performance computing systems can mimic human intelligence. AI excels at solving problems, finding patterns, and even making predictions at speeds far greater than human minds. If it is not combined with machine learning, then AI systems are confined to using a narrow, rules-based approach, which severely limits their flexibility. Fortunately, there are subsets of AI that allow an advanced system—like a digital human—to learn from new data and make more nuanced decisions.

There are multiple, interrelated aspects of AI at the heart of every data-intensive project, including the development of digital human agents.

Machine learning (or **ML**) is a subset of AI, dating back to the 1950s with things like Arthur Samuel's checkers-playing program. ML is based on the premise that ***computers should be able to learn without being explicitly programmed***. It allows AI systems to learn from experience—or rather, from the data—rather than being instructed how to respond to every scenario. Using a specified training dataset, ML algorithms can reveal the data's inherent patterns, rules, and relationships, using it to fine-tune and improve the program's performance. Ideally, when the data changes, the ML algorithms would also learn from that new data, adapting its responses to changing conditions. When a move in checkers resulted in a lost game, Samuel's program "learned" not to do that again. From that moment until now, ML algorithms have addressed far more complex situations, but the basic principle remains the same.

Machine learning requires a known training dataset in order to produce the desired results. The simplest form of this involves *structured data*—labeled information, like the numbers or words in a spreadsheet cell or a database record. In this basic ML approach, known as *supervised learning*, the correct answers are known; the algorithm simply learns to map inputs to outputs, improving its ability to predict as it is exposed to more and more examples. Automatic spam filters are a good example of this.

A more advanced ML approach, known as *unsupervised learning*, is designed to identify patterns in *unstructured data*—everything from images in a medical scan to unlabeled text or voice recordings. This does not require explicit guidance on what constitutes a "correct" answer in order to detect patterns, groupings, or anomalies. However, as many ChatGPT and facial recognition system users have discovered, ML-enabled AI programs do not really "know" what they are reading or seeing. Without human oversight, they can easily come up with bad answers. This is known as hallucinating, "where AI generates a convincing, contextually coherent but [*entirely fabricated response*] that is independent of the user's input or previous context."[1]

A third ML approach, *reinforcement learning*, is especially relevant when it comes to digital human agents. It is inspired in part by the behavioral psychology of B.F. Skinner and others, which holds that people tend to act in ways that avoid negative outcomes and result in positive ones. This "carrot and stick" approach to ML has been used successfully to train systems to excel at complex games like chess and Go—learning from mistakes and anticipating complex future scenarios.

For digital human agents, reinforcement learning occurs with each interaction with a human counterpart—and accumulates those experiences over time. When it receives a positive response from a human counterpart, the digital human "remembers" what it said or did to elicit that response and does so more often in future. When the response is negative, it tries to remedy the immediate problem and "remembers" to avoid it in future. Over multiple interactions, especially with familiar teammates, the digital human will seem more helpful and humanlike.

Remember, however, that this "hot and cold" ML method does not actually create a conscious awareness of good or bad behavior in the digital human agent: It is simply a means of classifying its human counterparts' actions and personal habit patterns, creating responses that facilitate a smooth-running team.

•——•

Deep Learning (or **DL**) is a branch of machine learning that has revolutionized the development of digital human agents. This refers to algorithms, particularly multilayered neural networks that mimic the way human brains process information. DL systems are good at processing *unstructured data*, including audio, images, and especially video. When designed properly, they can easily detect patterns in the data, classify them, and formulate appropriate responses.

In digital humans, DL is used to enhance speech recognition and visual interpretation. Unlike ChatGPT and other large language models, they are able to detect more nuances in spoken language, including slang, context, intent, and even emotional tone. Likewise, it can detect visual cues in a user's facial expressions or body language, enabling it to assign emotional significance to the conversation. For example, indications of confusion or frustration in the voice or face of a human counterpart would be the basis for a comforting or encouraging (and preferably helpful) response.

Later in the chapter, we'll see that deep learning also plays a part in generating a more humanlike visual and audible response. As a digital human agent learns to interpret the meanings of subtle human expression, it will be better able to simulate those subtle cues in response. In fact, the longer a digital human interacts with recognized human counterparts, the more personalized the experience will become.

Ears and Eyes

Many advanced AI and ML systems today simply connect with the necessary data directly, through their access to public and/or private data repositories. But a digital human "brain" also requires training data input from the human beings who work with it. Since the whole idea is to free us from manual data entry, the digital human agent must collect the data by itself. It must interpret what its human counterparts are saying and what they are expressing nonverbally. The two technologies for interacting audibly and visually with us humans are integral aspect of advanced, unsupervised machine learning.

Natural Language Processing (or **NLP**) is a familiar concept to anyone who has used ChatGPT, Perplexity, or any of the dozens of apps that convert queries and conversations into more or less coherent answers, transcripts, and summaries. It uses both machine learning and deep learning to process and then generate human language. Like all AI systems, NLP does *not* understand what it is hearing or saying the way a human being would. Rather, it uses advanced mathematical models to analyze and classify the words or sounds we make—all unstructured data—and then generate a written or audible response. Again, its response is not one of conscious understanding: it predicts what word(s) should follow logically after other words.

Given the vast complexity and nuances of human language,* it's a wonder that NLP-based systems can manage what they hear and say at all. But fortunately, such systems are becoming amazingly accurate.

A digital human can be like a helpful, knowledgeable human assistant, one who understands your requests and knows ways to meet them.

In digital humans, NLP involves several different components working together to create an experience approaching that of working with a real human. First, *automatic speech recognition* converts the user's spoken words into text format—a relatively simple task for today's AI models. Next, a separate module mathematically interprets the common meaning and intent behind the words, using basic rules to parse grammar, extract keywords, and "understand" the context of the conversation. Advanced digital humans also use ***large language models*** (or **LLMs**) to interpret what the user is asking.

Once the spoken input is interpreted, NLP is used again to generate a coherent response, often based on other relevant data, such as the user's previous history and preferences or other, general information about the organization or project. In practice, a well-implemented digital human is like a helpful, very knowledgeable human assistant who understands your requests and knows several ways to meet them. It can also remember what was said earlier in the conversation, avoiding repetitive responses—very much like an attentive human would do.

* To understand how complex it really is, see Samuel I. Hayakawa's 1941 book, *Language In Action*, which describes many of the human abstractions and unconscious assumptions that make verbal communication so difficult.

Modern NLP-enabled systems can do more than handle the literal words. They use a process called *sentiment analysis* to discern meaningful patterns associated with human emotion. This is often based on training data from many previous conversations, identifying positive and negative words, considering context and sentence structure, and calculating an overall "sentiment score"—positive, neutral, or negative. Some systems can even detect changes in tone that would indicate a change in the speaker's emotional state.

By "reading between the lines" in these ways, an NLP-enabled digital human can make the audible conversation feel effortless and natural for the user, bridging the psychological gap between humans and their digital teammates.

•——•

The visual component of our interaction with digital human agents is known as ***computer vision*** (or **CV**). In some ways, it's as old as digital scanners and barcodes—enabling computer systems to "see" visual elements that enter data or send users to an online destination. But computer vision has become infinitely more complex. Scanning a QR code involves only 4,200 static characters, at most. To scan and analyze a human face on HD video, a CV system must process up to sixty million pixels *per second*.

We already know CV as a way to securely access online banking or other sensitive apps on our phones. It is also widely used in facial recognition programs, despite the fact that these can unfairly target minorities.* Retailers also use it to monitor their store shelves, warehouses, and even customer traffic patterns. For digital human agents, computer vision systems are their eyes,

* Like all AI systems, computer vision is only as good as the training data it uses. In Chapter 6, we'll explore some of the risks of using digital human agents, including bias in the data.

collecting and decoding the world around them—especially the faces of their human counterparts.

Computer vision, when combined with deep learning, gives a digital human agent the ability to "read" human facial expressions accurately and respond appropriately.

A digital human is typically equipped with a digital camera, similar to a typical HD webcam (in many cases, it may actually *be* the human user's webcam or built-in phone camera). Behind the scenes, the camera's raw visual data goes through a noise reduction and enhancement process before being sent to a ***convolutional neural network*** (or **CNN**), a fairly recent deep learning model made possible by ultrafast processor hardware. This AI model identifies edges and textures in the data, learning to recognize complex objects, spatial relationships, and of course contextual information. This information is paired with NLP and sentiment analysis which gives the digital human the ability to "read" its human counterparts' facial expressions accurately and respond appropriately.

The Soul of a Machine?

For many years, fiction writers have speculated that computers will "wake up" someday, to either help or harm their human makers. But even when ***artificial general intelligence*** (or **AGI**) becomes a reality in the next fifteen to thirty-five years,[2] the chances are that harm is far more likely to come about through poor implementation or malicious action (as we'll cover in Chapter 5) than it is through AI systems becoming self-aware.

Today, artificial intelligence, and the digital humans it enables, are not capable of literal emotion or empathy. However, they are becoming increasingly capable of recognizing and simulating emotional responses, a branch of artificial intelligence known as ***emotion AI***[3] or ***affective computing***. Pioneered by Rosalind Picard at the MIT Media Lab, the field is a combination of psychology, neuroscience, and computer science.

Emotion AI uses a variety of techniques besides sentiment analysis to discern people's emotional states and expressions. These include large language models, eye tracking, gestures, and the controversial technique of facial coding of expressions to infer emotion in a subject.

In some cases, emotion AI can have difficulty identifying emotions from complex datasets. And, like other facets of artificial intelligence, it is subject to potential bias, especially if the training dataset is skewed by racial, gender, culture, or disability stereotypes. There are also privacy concerns and a lack of current legal safeguards. It has been used successfully in mental healthcare situations, monitoring the emotional well-being of patients. Most notably, however, it is being used in customer service situations, enhancing the user experience by adapting responses based on simple emotional cues.

Creating a Digital Human Body

We human beings prefer to interact with each other visually; that's how we survived for thousands of years. Relatively recent inventions like the telephone have made it easier to interact by voice alone, even over long distances, but deep down we still prefer face-to-face contact. So, it's no wonder we want our digital human teammates to have a voice *and* a face.

To embody a digital human—how it appears and moves on screen—requires the very latest and most powerful application of computer graphics, starting with 3D modeling. Artists, aided by scanning systems and predesigned 3D wireframe "building blocks," first create a model of a human figure, complete with facial features, body shape, skin texture, and hair. Much of the latter can be acquired via high-resolution scans of actual human subjects and then "mapped" onto the 3D wireframes, even including wrinkles and blemishes. These figures are mostly familiar human *types*, but in some cases, they can also be the "digital twins" of an actual human being. This of course requires more effort and skill on the part of artists and 3D technicians.

The next step is animation and rendering, arguably the most processor-intensive computing task in creating a digital human. We are used to seeing realistic, emotionally engaging characters in films like *Avatar*. However, what few realize is that after these models are created, and their motion captured from live actors wearing sensors, it requires many hours of computer time to render the final animated sequences. This can limit, at least for now, the range of motion and the detail a moving digital human can display in real time.

Increasingly, however, digital humans *can* manage a wide range of facial expressions and subtle movements that create a realistic human appearance. Much of this is powered by the same deep learning AI and sentiment analysis that allows a digital human to "know" their human counterparts' emotional state. Similar to the cues you expect in a Zoom or Teams meeting, digital human agents can nod, smile, blink, simulate eye contact, and many other motions and gestures that foster engagement. Studies have shown that humans pay closer attention and have a greater sense of affinity when interacting with a lifelike digital character, compared with an animated, cartoonlike avatar.[4]

Must Digital Humans Be Seen?

Much ado has been made of the uncanny valley effect that some digital human agents have evoked. Limited by graphics processing speeds, these not quite human looking agents can potentially make people uncomfortable. But that phenomenon may be short-lived, as we grow accustomed to working with

digital teammates, and especially as their *proficiency* in handling routine matters improves.

Research suggests that our perceptions of digital human agents are also changing. In one study, when participants were led to believe that the agent was controlled by AI, researchers found no difference in their responses to actual humans and digital humans.[5]

Eventually, improvements in high-performance computing will make AI-enabled digital humans far more lifelike and less robotic in appearance. But also keep in mind that these digital teammates do not have to be visible at all times or in every situation. Just as our communication with human teammates is a mix of face-to-face and virtual meetings, phone calls, and emails, so too our digital counterparts can work with us on many levels, not just on screen.

Thanks to exponential growth in AI, graphics, and communication technology, our helpful digital assistants can work with us "in person," over the phone, and through email, texts, and chat. They will also remember how and when we prefer to hear from them. In the future, digital human agents may also be embodied in anthropomorphic robots, which is beyond the scope of this book. But for now, these human-appearing digital teammates, on a screen or otherwise, have enormous potential to make our work and our lives better.

Putting It All Together: Human-Computer Interaction

Even with advances in AI, machine learning, and motion graphics, a digital human project can falter if it's not designed with the end user in mind. ***Human-Computer Interaction*** (or **HCI**) is the discipline that ensures the technology actually connects with users in a natural, intuitive way. It covers user experience (or **UX**) design and the use of *multimodal* interfaces that allow users to interact with the digital human through multiple channels, such as voice, text, and visual cues. In essence, HCI for digital humans is about crafting the *conversation flow, personality, and interface* such that users feel comfortable and engaged.

One key aspect of HCI is the *persona* of the digital human. Just as a customer service representative is trained on tone and etiquette, a digital human's character and behavior need to be *designed*. Should it be formal and professional—or friendly and humorous? Are its words and manner consistent with the type of organization it represents? HCI defines how the digital human greets users, how it handles turn taking in a conversation, and even how it creates facial expressions and hand gestures at critical moments. These design choices can make an interaction enjoyable instead of awkward. A well-designed digital human will use appropriate *body language*—such as a nod to indicate it's listening, or a smile to put a user at ease—based on what is natural in human conversations.

Another critical part of HCI in this context is handling *multimodal interaction*. This means that the user can communicate not just via voice, but also by clicking options, typing, or using gestures, and the digital human can respond accordingly. For instance, if the digital human is on a kiosk with a touch screen, the UX might offer clickable prompts in addition to spoken dialogue. Or if the camera is on, the system might detect a user's facial expressions. Designing a cohesive experience means deciding when the digital human should speak versus displaying text, which is important in noisy environments. It means deciding how it should signal that it's thinking, possibly using a subtle animation while the AI computes a response, in order to avoid user impatience. It also means planning how to gracefully handle misunderstandings or interruptions. HCI best practices are intended to guide these details so that the interaction feels smooth.

Ultimately, HCI ties together the tech components into a user-facing experience. Here, a prime measure of success is how *natural* the interaction feels. Because digital humans interpret multimodal human cues like facial expression, tone of voice, and words, they can respond in ways that feel natural and personalized. For business leaders, good HCI design means higher user adoption and satisfaction. People will actually want to use the digital human interface because it is both intuitive and pleasant as well as practical and efficient.

Future Technologies and Digital Humans

The technologies described above are what make digital human agents possible. These are being improved almost daily, but the next generation of data and internet technologies has the potential to accelerate agentic AI even further. While they pose elements of risk (as all technology does), they also set the stage for a future where our digital allies are aligned more closely and effectively with human values and autonomy.

The most significant of these is Web3, an array of internet technologies designed to distribute and "[...]disperse power, authority, and control away from a central location."[6] An integral component of Web3 is *blockchain*, a secure, decentralized digital "ledger" of transactions spanning multiple computers. Blockchain has a bad public reputation, thanks to abuses of its most familiar byproducts, cryptocurrency. But the technology itself has great potential "[...]for storing data in a way that is nearly impossible to fake."[7]

The implications are revolutionary. Even as digital agents show greater ability to learn, making them more and more humanlike, industries have shied away from expanding their roles, fearing a loss of control. But blockchain changes that dynamic. It provides the necessary transparency and transaction security, allowing AI agents (including digital humans) to connect and learn from one another, and to do so safely, autonomously, and at scale.[8]

A second, more familiar future technology, the ***Internet of Things*** (or **IoT**), also holds great promise for expanding the roles and capabilities of AI-enabled agents. A digital human's "eyes" are the many ways it receives information, both from existing data sources and from the words and actions of its human counterparts. But they also need input from devices that humans use in their work. As these devices become more capable of communicating, their sensors can provide AI agents with contextual data, helping them make decisions in real time. For example, a digital human assistant in a hospital environment would know the current vital statistics of a patient, as well as their treatment history, making it better able to collaborate with a human physician.

There are still barriers to adoption, of course. Web3 and blockchain interfaces are still relatively user-unfriendly, which will slow mainstream embracement. Also, these technologies have high energy and computational requirements. But at the end of the day, they will elevate digital humans to a whole new level.

Each of the technologies described in this chapter has its own intrinsic value. In fact, many organizations already use machine learning, deep learning, and other tools to create other AI solutions for cost savings and new business growth. For them, creating digital humans is simply the next step.

A well-designed digital human agent is greater than the sum of all its parts. Without AI, it would not have a brain; without NLP and computer vision, it would be deaf and blind; without advanced graphics, it would not have a face; and without good HCI design, it would confuse and discourage its users. But with each of those elements engaged, and with ethical and sustainable principles in place, digital humans can empower their human partners to do bigger and greater things than they ever thought possible.

CHAPTER 3

Defining the Digital Human Advantage

Artificial intelligence has been generating a ***lot*** of buzz in the months since the "early days" of ChatGPT.* Much of it has been hyperbolic, raising all sorts of wild speculation—both good and bad. But what if AI had a human face, a voice, and a personality? What if it could emulate the look, sound, and feel of a real human ally—and at the same time be *genuinely helpful* in our day-to-day lives?

In later chapters, we'll discuss the potential for harm and misuse—and how to avoid it. But in this chapter, let's examine how these digital human agents are already changing the game in five key industries: customer service, healthcare, finance, education, and retail. In each case, digital humans can enhance our experience and increase our productivity. Early adopters in these fields are already seeing the benefits, leading some to

* For those who don't remember that far back, ChatGPT-3.5 came out in late 2022.

predict that most managers will be working alongside a digital human colleague or assistant—probably more than one—within a few years.

Well-planned and implemented digital humans never tire. They never experience burnout, and they don't complain or ask for more pay or time off. They are ready and able to help. When they make mistakes, as all assistants do, they do not sulk or seek ways to undermine those who correct them. A digital human agent is always on call, any time of day or night. Their sole mission is to fill in the gaps and make your lives better.

As with all forms of AI, digital human agents can be created in ways that minimize or eliminate bias—which is more than we can say of human beings. But perhaps most importantly, digital humans represent the potential for *psychological* benefits. Adding a human face, voice, and mannerisms to AI makes the interactions *feel* more real. Even when we know they are artificial, our minds can more easily become attuned to them. We can connect with them emotionally as well as practically, creating a profound change in the nature of work.

May I Be of Service?

It's ten o'clock on Friday night. Alex was all set to watch a documentary on Netflix, but the Wi-Fi has failed. There's good news and bad news: His phone has a 5G connection, so he can look up the FAQ pages for the router; unfortunately, they go on forever. Frustrated, he clicks the support chat and is greeted immediately by a courteous virtual agent, Mia. "Hi Alex. I see you're having internet problems. Let's see how I can help." For the next few minutes, Mia walks Alex through the process of resetting and testing the router. Her instructions are simple, including clear visuals. When he gets mixed up, Mia rephrases in a patient, sympathetic tone, with facial expressions to match. By the end of the exchange, the router is up and running. Alex knew he was working with an AI-driven agent, not a real person. At the same time, he marveled at the levels of empathy and practical help he received during the interaction.

•———•

This scene illustrates how digital humans like Mia can be used to reinvent ***customer service***. It's a problem we've struggled to overcome. When life was less complicated, and when we bought more goods and services locally, it was easier to talk live with a human being who knew who we were and could help fix any problems. But as our world got faster and more complex, the ideal of "24-7 support" got harder and harder to meet. Human agents can't be on call every hour of the day, especially if the company is small and/or budgets are tight. Offshore call centers are largely script driven and impersonal. Even when there are empathetic, knowledgeable customer support people, waiting on hold for "the next available agent" seems like an eternity.

On the other hand, a digital human customer service rep ***can*** be immediately available, at any time of the day or night—with zero time spent on hold. Digital humans can be unfailingly sympathetic and supportive, navigating both the problem at hand *and* the frustration or confusion of their human counterpart. This scenario achieves several business goals simultaneously. First, the problem itself is addressed, ensuring the longevity of the product or service. Second, the customer experience is decidedly positive, making their loyalty to the brand even stronger. Third, if the agent is well designed, each customer service exchange provides valuable data to the designers, helping them create even better products and services in the future. In the long run, it saves on the cost of customer service, but it offers other long-term benefits for growth and improvement.

Bank You Very Much

Beginning in 2017, the Royal Bank of Scotland, a NatWest Group subsidiary, tested a lifelike digital avatar, Cora, to help customers with basic queries and give its digital banking initiative "[...] a more human face."[1] The bank had reduced the number of local branches and had announced job cuts but decided to deploy the new technology only if Cora passed her probationary period.

The digital teller, wearing a NatWest uniform and a stylish ear piercing, answered simple questions like how to apply for a mortgage or what to do if the customer lost a debit card.

"'Testing has suggested customers that have avoided digital services in the past may be more inclined to interact with digital humans like Cora,' a spokesperson with NatWest explained. "'The technology has real potential for the future and we're also looking at how we can use it to help train our staff[...].'"[2]

Since its introduction, some users have expressed frustration with Cora's responsiveness and reliability. However, as a generative AI service, it has achieved an impressive accuracy rate of 98.5 percent. The developers are hoping to reach even greater accuracy—so long as it can be done without taking undue risks.[3]

Researchers have found that, when it comes to taking customers through complex tasks or dealing with emotionally charged issues, digital humans significantly outperform text-based chatbots. In a recent *Harvard Business Review* research report,[4] the findings found that a traditional text interface such as a chatbot is preferred for quick interactions, but a digital human can do a much better job communicating complex instructions and emotionally engaging with a customer. They also work well in a situation where the customer isn't sure what they want and is open to exploring options.

There are drawbacks to a one-size-fits-all approach. The trend is clear, however. By combining empathy with endless patience, digital humans are turning customer service from a cost center into an opportunity to reduce costs and build customer loyalty. They can deliver helpful information in a way that's both efficient and humane.

Compassionate Healthcare, Virtually Delivered

In a remote, rural town, Maria has managed to live largely on her own, thanks to convenient delivery services and occasional visits from kind neighbors and friends. As an elderly woman, however, she suffers from ailments that require frequent monitoring. Her primary care physician has these issues well in hand but cannot monitor her progress regularly, even over Zoom. Enter Molly, a digital companion/nurse who appears each morning on Maria's screen. After the usual greeting, she asks, "How are you feeling today?" With infinite patience, Molly listens to her concerns with appropriate expressions of empathy—how well she slept, how her knees are feeling, or anything new or different. Behind the scenes, Molly interprets all the new data and adds it to Maria's overall history, flagging anything that a human doctor might find anomalous or concerning. During the session, Molly gives Maria gentle, helpful reminders on taking medication or doing light exercises recommended for her condition. The call ends on a pleasant note. Maria knows Molly is digital, but she's comfortable knowing that she will be there tomorrow.

In multiple healthcare fields, digital human agents are beginning to serve as caregivers, medical assistants, and even therapists. Here, the emphasis is not so much about cost saving—although it is economical. Rather, they serve to extend the *reach* of medical professionals, providing support (and gathering valuable data) in ways that feel personal. Patients know they are dealing with a proxy, but the digital human can fill a deeper, psychological need—especially if the responses are actually helpful.

Besides routine medical monitoring, digital humans are advancing the practice of mental health counselling and therapy. Traditionally, the limited ability of licensed therapists to meet with veterans in person forced them to rely more on surveys. This makes it difficult to identify PTSD and the potential for suicides. But in a 2017 study, researchers found that soldiers were more likely to open up about their post-traumatic stress when interviewed by a virtual interviewer than by taking a survey.[5]

More recently, Iowa State Professor Lingyao Yuan noted that veterans were more likely to disclose their PTSD symptoms to digital humans than they were to real-life medical professionals.[6] This aligns with other findings, where digital humans facilitated greater symptom disclosure because of their ability to build rapport while also maintaining anonymity.

The digital human advantage in healthcare lies in the ability to provide consistent accessible and scalable assistance, while also making it empathetic. Digital human agents, properly designed, make the experience feel more personal and supportive, collecting crucial information while also easing the workload of primary care professionals.

Money Matters in the Digital World

Priya is a Gen Z professional with a promising career. She has some savings and a generous 401(k) plan. Her financial advisor has planned wisely, helping her invest in a diverse portfolio. But after a long day, she is unsettled by the constant flood of stock market news on her phone. She's planning to buy a car, so she needs to get some sound advice. But she's not nearly important enough (or obnoxious enough) to call her advisor and demand an after-hours meeting. Instead, she opens her banking app and is greeted by Aria, a digital human advisor. "Good evening, Priya," she says. "What's on your mind?" She might also add, "Would you like to go over your budget and investment goals?" Over the next half hour, they chat about her worries about the market, and the prospects for buying a car. Aria walks her through the long-term health and history of her portfolio, notes her good spending and saving history, and points her to the first steps in applying for a loan. If Priya's voice or expression betrays any anxiety, Aria gently offers to clarify or repeat. Priya feels confident by the end of the session. It felt like talking to a knowledgeable friend or colleague, except that Aria is available anytime, day or night—and has all her confidential information at hand.

In the volatile world of banking and finance, digital humans are being deployed as assistant financial advisors, customer service reps, and online bank tellers. Unlike their human counterparts, digital agents do not require sleep and can jump in at any time of the day or night. They are also not subject to our unconscious, subjective feelings of fear or panic over market conditions, so long as their AI training data are screened for bias. Customers do not need to spend time on hold, or put up with rote, half-informed answers. The AI persona can provide reliable information instantly.

What a well-designed digital human *can* do is respond in an empathetic, relatable manner, detecting emotional cues, and responding in the moment to complex questions. In addition, as with the healthcare example, a virtual human financial agent *must be completely trustworthy*, using the client's financial data in strict confidence. All new information acquired in conversations with the digital human can only be shared with its human fiduciary, with the client's interests first.

Naturally, the sources of a digital human's answers on financial matters (like those from any AI system) must be strictly vetted, not scraped from the vast, and often unreliable internet at large. Like its human counterpart, a digital human in the financial sector cannot be a mysterious "black box;" transparency is an absolute requirement. The user must have confidence that its answers are founded in reality.

Personalized Learning Companions

Max is a friendly, cartoonlike online learning buddy for Sam, a ten-year-old student without access to personal tutors. When Sam struggles with his math homework, Max doesn't give him the answers: He senses Sam's frustration and offers both encouragement and interactive visuals—like a pizza divided into slices as an illustration for fractions.

In another home, the digital human learning assistant is no longer Max, the friendly teen. For high school student Maria, its persona is that of a patient, older teacher who helps her review a biology assignment. This virtual tutor adapts each lesson based on Maria's progress—going quickly when she grasps a concept easily and slowing down to revisit topics she finds difficult.

Both of these digital human personas are infinitely patient, and available when even the best human teachers are sound asleep. Both Sam and Maria know they're working with a digital human, but both feel more engaged and confident, as if they each had an amazing private tutor.

Individualized learning, like the one-room schoolhouse, is a next to impossible goal today. Constrained by hard economics and the pressure to produce good test results, schools are forced to adopt a one-size-fits-all model—an approach that has failed spectacularly for decades.[7] The problem is, as much as we aspire to adapt curriculum to the needs and progress of the learner, there are simply not enough people and dollars to manage it for non-wealthy individuals.

Educators are realizing the potential of AI to resolve this dilemma, moving us towards a practical approach to adaptive learning.[8] A key element of this solution involves the development of digital agents capable of presenting relevant content and adapting the pace and tone to meet individual students' progress and needs.

An analysis by McKinsey & Company found that individualized learning made possible by AI-powered learning programs can boost student engagement by up to 60 percent while increasing educational results by 30 percent.[9] Similarly, US Department of Education research indicates that AI-powered tutoring systems can raise student achievement levels to the same level as one-on-one tutoring,[10] although the same report cautioned that unequal access to technology (the digital divide) will impact the total results.

Like their counterparts in customer service, healthcare, and financial services, digital human education assistants are available at all hours, to anyone with a secure connection to the school's learning system. Given the complex nature of learning—especially the personalized variety—these agents will not replace their human teacher and professor counterparts; rather, they will extend their reach and their capabilities with limitless knowledge and patience. They will ensure that no student will be forced to learn alone, even when human help is unavailable or unaffordable.

The Immersive Shopping Experience

From her small apartment, Keiko is shopping online for a new outfit. Tired of watching endless influencers on TikTok, she opens a fashion retailer's mobile app and is greeted by two charming digital humans, Ren and Rin. Keiko tells them her measurements—or lets them use a 3D scan—and Rin (the female avatar) adjusts accordingly. After chatting about style and color preferences, Keiko picks an outfit and Rin tries it on. She can see it from all angles and in different lighting—accompanied by helpful style comments from both Ren and Rin. Alternatives and accessories are discussed and, once her decision is made, a helpful digital clerk arrives to complete the purchase, to Keiko's utter satisfaction.

•——•

This fictional example is modeled after an emerging retail trend in Japan that is poised to transform the retail industry as a whole. In this case, digital human sales associates extend the retailer's reach, helping shoppers visualize clothing and accessories as a prelude to e-commerce purchases.

Digital humans fulfill several needs in the retail world. Engaging customers at the point of sale has always been an essential part of the equation, but with the decline of brick-and-mortar stores, and the subsequent rise in e-commerce, that personal touch is conspicuously missing. Even when in-store interactions are possible, many sales associates lack the essential skills for those roles. By some estimates, over two-thirds of sales representatives have contemplated leaving their positions due to inadequate training practices from their managers.

Using digital humans in retail will not replace human sales associates, but they can help better train them, at any time and at a significant savings over in person training. Moreover, they can go where human salespeople cannot—into the virtual world of today's shopper.

Digital e-commerce has long relied on custom shopping apps, SEO, and social media to drive sales. But responsive, AI-driven digital humans are more likely to provide a meaningful experience than any other automated channel. They are more likely to extend the customer's interaction—beyond their initial search. As Hai Li, the cofounder and CEO of developer Pinscreen explained,

"You want the customer to [explore] how things [like clothes] could be, and how they might like them to look. From a user experience standpoint, you want to keep them engaged and able to explore the brand."

The Digital Human Advantage in Everyday Life

As these examples show, the digital human advantage is not about replacing humans with machines. On the contrary, it is about ***extending human capacity*** and making interactions with technology more natural and meaningful.

- For customer service professionals, digital humans amplify their core knowledge of products or services and extend their reach beyond normal business hours. For their customers, digital humans provide a more empathetic, helpful connection at any time of the day—solving problems and strengthening their affinity for the brand. The relationship does result in lower costs, but it also creates value beyond greater efficiency.
- For the healthcare provider, digital humans allow them to give more patients personalized, companion-like care—on a continuing basis and at a reasonable cost. Data from these engagements gives the provider a much more comprehensive view of the patient's progress for when they do interact directly.
- For financial planners and fiduciaries, digital humans apply their knowledge of clients' investments, and of current market conditions and trends, to provide personalized, empathetic support at all hours. While humans still control the core objectives, digital human agents help democratize financial literacy and provide greater peace of mind.
- For educators, digital humans are an invaluable online tutor and study assistant, giving students the kind of

engaging, personalized attention they need but often cannot afford.

- For online retailers and even some traditional retail stores, digital humans can serve as a personal shopper or guide, providing a personal touch that will facilitate sales and improve brand loyalty.

In these examples and more, digital humans can build ***constructive empathy at scale***—that is when they are designed responsibly. They listen, adapt, and remember, creating a connection that feels genuine. Although the user knows the digital human isn't real, they are nevertheless emotionally attuned to facial signals and gestures—connecting instinctively without having to become computer experts.[11]

In terms of productivity, digital human agents allow us to ***do more with less***, taking on the heavy listing of routine interactions, freeing up human experts and teams to tackle complex, creative, or high-empathy tasks. A doctor can focus on a complex diagnosis while a digital assistant monitors and interacts with stable patients. A teacher can spend extra time to mentor those who need extra help while a digital tutor makes sure other class members are keeping up with assignments—and directs them to other resources as they learn. In these and many other scenarios, digital humans add to the organization's net value; they do not take value away.

There are challenges and ethical questions, of course, as we'll explore in Chapter 5, but the reality is that digital human agents, like the AI technology that powers them, have the ability to work alongside us to create a smarter, kinder, and more productive world.

CHAPTER 4

The Digital Human Ecosystem

To many people, artificial intelligence systems seem magical. In response to a well-worded prompt, a ***large language model*** (or LLM) can synthesize a human-sounding answer of any length or style, at breathtaking speeds. In response to additional prompts, it can also fine-tune its responses and even identify sources—even if those sources are fictitious.[1] AI image and video generators seem magical as well, conjuring new pixels from existing ones on request. This "magic" is what's known as ***generative AI***—one of many aspects of every digital human. But the key thing to remember is that generative AI systems ***cannot act on their own***. They must have human input and instruction; from the data it is fed, to the parameters it must follow. If a digital human was based entirely on generative AI, it would be like an unwieldy puppet, requiring constant intervention and control.

Long before ChatGPT and Copilot dominated the news, generative AI was a well-accepted part of the information technology landscape. For years, data scientists and programmers used large datasets to find meaningful patterns and predict future probabilities. With recent technology advances, we can now build AI models that generate results even faster. It's true that digital humans must be able to assimilate vast datasets and generate responses. But effective digital humans must be much more than just rapid data handlers.

Agentic AI is not limited to passive content creation; it can proactively complete tasks, put them in context, and even learn from experience.

A more recent development, called ***agentic AI***, provides the ability to take actions *independently* in order to achieve specific goals. Those goals are set by humans, as they should be, but an agentic system can make decisions, execute tasks, adapt to changing environments, and interact with other systems (and with actual humans) ***without constant human guidance***. It is not limited to passive content creation; it can proactively complete tasks, put them in context, and even learn from experience. For example, a *generative* AI system can draft an email; an *agentic* AI can decide when to send it, schedule a follow-up appointment, and put that email exchange into a larger business context for future decision making. It can make decisions *autonomously*. The difference is, generative AI can create content that mimics human creativity, while agentic AI takes actions to achieve specific, desirable goals.[2]

Digital human agents are a combination of both types of artificial intelligence. They generate responses—text, sound, and visuals—from a vast dataset, but one that is being constantly updated in real time. Their data includes not only relevant, traditional business information—like that used by any generative AI system—but also information derived from facial expressions, tonal variance, and other cues.

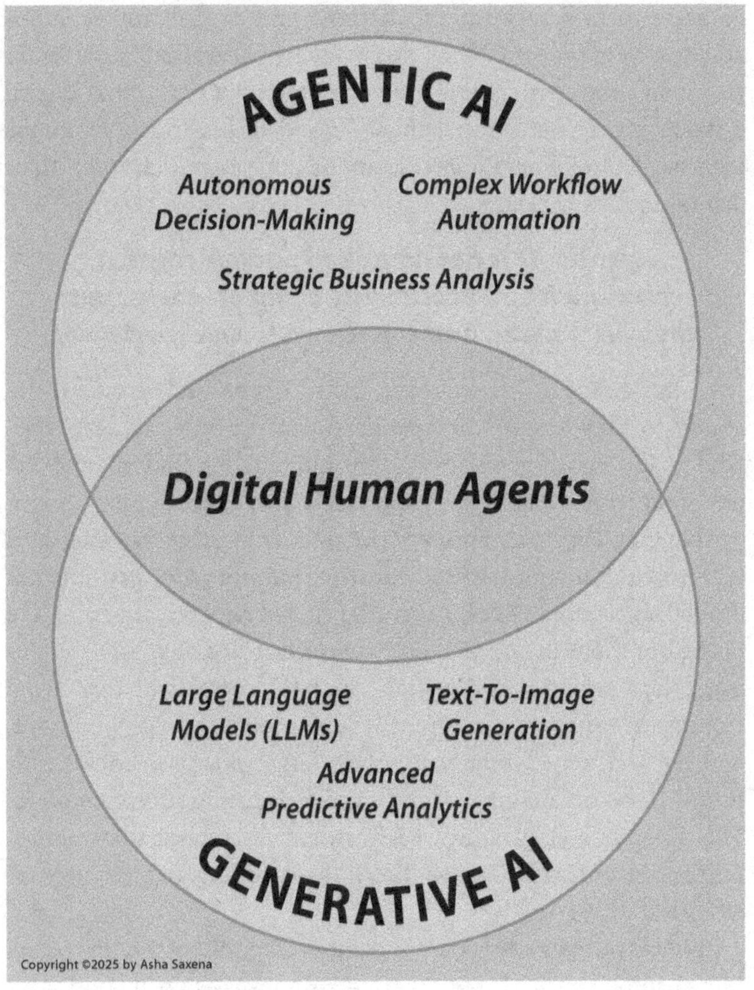

Digital humans are at the intersection of generative and agentic artificial intelligence.

Agentic AI systems also require a clearly defined goal—one that come from humans with needs and vision. Once a goal or purpose is established, and all the necessary data is made available, such a system can make decisions on its own. Those autonomous decisions can range from a humanlike response to an unexpected question, all the way to performing routine tasks, recording the results, and learning to improve its performance the next time. Collaboration and oversight by humans are still essential, but a digital human agent does not need to wait around constantly for input before doing its job.

The Future of Work

Charlene Li is an author, keynote speaker, and founder of the Quantum Networks Group, helping business leaders take advantage of the disruption potential of artificial intelligence. In a recent interview, she outlined some of the basic aspects of digital humans—and how they'll affect the way we work.

Part of the challenge is in the way people are viewing the technology today. "Organizations are inherently uncomfortable with uncertainty," she said, "but the rise of AI—especially agentic AI—requires a new approach." Rather than merely taking steps to remove uncertainty, Li maintained, business leaders should be asking if their organization has the flexibility required to use these new agents.

Digital humans should be considered not just as a tool, like a computer that always requires input. Rather, Li noted that they should be viewed as "true digital workers," capable of functioning on their own. If they are charged with the right goal, or tasked with making sure things don't "go haywire," then we should be able to trust them. They should also be able to learn along the way, as if to say, "Here's a situation I haven't seen before. I'll try several new things and see if any of them work here."

Li emphasizes the importance of explicit objectives, not only in the creation of digital human agents themselves but also as the basis for continuous learning and performance measurement. "The number one thing is to be very clear about your business objectives, your management objectives, and your performance objectives."

Of course, these objectives must align with the company's core goals and values. "The risk is that you don't train them well," Li continued. "Problems will occur if you just throw them into a situation, without safeguards, hoping they'll work out—but without putting enough thought into what you really want them to do."

She was equally clear about the best technological approach to creating effective digital humans. "The key to building any sort of tech stack in AI is to be super flexible," she observed. "The agentic learning algorithms you build are unique to your business but the models you use to run them are not. So, if you build a digital human agent to run on top of, say, OpenAI or Gemini, make sure it can also run on any other platform, so you can use the best model that comes along. Your agent needs to know where to get the data, how to recognize and solve the problem, and how to decide if the answer was good or not."

Li asserted that AI-enabled agents can actually make us better as human beings, by providing feedback that helps us identify and address bias and improve our interpersonal skills. "Honestly, we're not very good at that." In the ideal ecosystem of digital and actual humans working together, we may find new ways of managing each other.

An ecosystem is defined as, "the complex of living organisms, their physical environment, and all their interrelationships in a particular unit of space."[3] Digital humans are not "living organisms," as far as we know, but they do inhabit a physical environment—mainly the cloud and our many devices. They're also interrelated to one another and to us, via the data they consume, the information they provide, and the actions they take in pursuit of our goals. So, to better understand the nature of our digital human counterparts, let's explore the three major "species" of digital humans.

Digital Human Assistants

The most familiar type of digital human is one that is designed to help humans accomplish tasks more effectively, answer questions, and otherwise facilitate our work and personal lives. Think of them as a capable concierge that makes everything run more smoothly, or as a capable customer service rep, or as an eager (and very adept) intern. They are available at any hour of the day or night, they can find answers in a flash, and they are never offended or hurt if they don't get everything just right—or if you're too busy to respond. They are able to anticipate your needs and, when they do make a mistake, they can learn from experience and do better the next time.

Digital human assistants are invaluable in customer-facing roles, as described in Chapter 1, but they also play an important role in teams of business professionals. They are not limited to a single location or time zone, so they can facilitate the work of every team member *simultaneously*—even when they are in locations all over the world. In this capacity, they would replace human interns or assistants,* but their value goes beyond saving on salary costs.

Human interns work for very low pay or no pay, either to earn school credit or to burnish their resumes. Entry-level assistants also tend to be on the low end of the pay scale. But even when they perform well, they are unlikely to keep on doing the same low-paying jobs. When they leave or move up the company ladder, their experience and institutional knowledge often goes with them. Their replacements must be retrained.

This is not the case with digital humans: They won't quit, and their knowledge of the team and its processes will only grow over time. Their value is less about cost savings and more

* In the next chapter, we'll address the issue of job displacement resulting from the use of digital humans.

about improving workflow and retaining the team's institutional knowledge.

Digital human assistants do not always need to be visible on screen. Like their human counterparts, they can participate as a voice or as a text-only message or email thread.

A digital human's on-screen presence is valuable, especially when emotional engagement is a priority. However, a digital assistant does not need an on-screen presence at all times. Just as a human intern or assistant can interact without being visible, a digital assistant can participate on a team as a voice or as a text-only message or email thread. Organizations can start out with an unseen digital human and add a visible avatar when it makes the most sense.

Digital human assistants can remember everything in their training data. They not only see all that data in context, they can also supplement the data in real time, based on changing conditions and interactions with each user. They can learn from the data and make many decisions without explicit instructions. When given clear objectives, they have the potential to greatly reduce costs, improve processes, and free their human counterparts to innovate and grow.

Hearing, Seeing, and Acting More Human

Whenever a digital human assistant is called upon to interact both visually and audibly, they rely on the core technologies detailed in Chapter 2. For the audible aspect, these include ***natural language processing*** (or NLP) used to classify and interpret the meaning of their teammate's spoken words. Conversely, the assistant also uses NLP to translate its response in a realistic manner. An advanced AI technology, ***natural language understanding*** (or NLU) is also required in order to parse the human user's intent.

For example, if you say, "I'm locked out of my account," the assistant's NLP/NLU capabilities can infer that you need help with a password reset—without having to hear a specific request.

The visual requirements for a digital human assistant vary with each situation. For a customer service rep or sales assistant, the appearance must be sufficiently humanlike to meet their counterpart's need for an emotional connection and the confidence that inspires. Reading nonverbal cues and responding appropriately are important steps towards greater engagement—and avoiding the "uncanny valley" problem. To do this, an assistant uses several technologies simultaneously:

- ***Computer vision and sentiment analysis:*** This is the AI/ML process designed to identify the speaker, detect visual cues from the video feed, and assign those cues a "sentiment score." From this data, the digital human assistant can "see" their counterpart, interpret their nonverbal cues, and, with repeated interactions, learn how to respond appropriately.
- ***3D modeling, animation, and rendering:*** As detailed in Chapter 2, this involves creating a visual appearance, including motions and gestures, that are human enough in appearance to foster productive engagement.

Another essential component of digital human assistants are their ability to maintain context—in a single conversation or over the entire course of meeting their primary objective. If you ask, "What's the weather like in Dallas?" and follow up with, "How about tomorrow?," the assistant must use ***dialog state tracking*** and its short-term memory of recent interactions to infer that the speaker is still talking about Dallas. If the context is larger, such as the speaker's company's business relationship with a particular client, the agent must be able to access ***customer relationship***

management (or CRM) and communication data in order to respond and take actions correctly.

> ***A digital human assistant can learn from successive encounters, detecting patterns of behavior and adjusting its responses and suggestions accordingly.***

Personalization is also a key aspect of an effective digital human assistant. Besides recognizing the speaker's identity, a good assistant will learn from successive encounters, detecting patterns of behavior and adjusting its responses and suggestions accordingly. For example, it might notice that you frequently talk to your mother on Sunday evenings. From that pattern, it could ask on Saturday if you want to set up a Zoom call, set it up in your calendar, send her the invitation, and gently remind you before the call starts. A digital human financial advisor or fitness coach could do the same—at a frequency and timing that suits your needs.

Connecting the Dots

A digital human assistant must have access to a wide range of other information systems, just as a good concierge has a comprehensive list of every conceivable resource a traveler might need. But the advantage a digital human has over a human concierge or assistant is significant. Once acquired, the digital list of resources is far less likely to be lost or forgotten, whereas the human assistant's list is more likely to be lost if they leave for another position—even if the list of resources is on a computer. A digital human assistant remembers not only the basic contact information, but also how and when it can best be used.

It's tempting to believe that such a well-connected digital human assistant would eliminate the need for a human equivalent—and thus, the jobs of entry-level assistants or concierges. It's true that some job loss will occur, but it is also true that a digital human assistant will make their human counterparts much more effective.

The key to connecting digital human assistants with an array of data sources and applications is the use of their ***application programming interfaces*** (or APIs). These are the rule sets, protocols, and tools that facilitate communication between different applications and systems. While there is no singular way to create or evaluate an API, there are some basic characteristics to look for:

- ***Consistency:*** A good API uses consistent, logical naming conventions. Wherever possible, it must also use standardized HTTP methods and status codes indicating success or errors.
- ***Ease of Use and Documentation:*** An API should be simple and intuitive, making it easy to understand without external guidance or long, complex documentation.
- ***Performance:*** The API, like the system it represents, should be able to handle high traffic without a degradation in performance. It should also be flexible accommodating multiple integration scenarios and data formats. Of course, it should also be highly secure, using robust authentication and encryption.
- ***Design:*** This is not referring to aesthetics, but to engineering norms like the RESTful design principles first published in 2000.[4]

A digital human assistant need not connect with every possible data source or application, of course, but only those required to fulfill its primary objective. A banking or customer service assistant might need connections to only a handful of resources. A virtual travel agent or hotel chain concierge would need connections to more resources from a wide range of external providers.

In a team or workgroup environment, the digital human assistant must have access to company databases, emails, recorded conversations, documents, and more. But no matter how many data sources are needed, each one must be robust, scalable, and secure.

Real-World Examples

There are many examples of digital human assistants in use today, although many of these are voice or text based only. The many all-purpose ***personal assistants*** like Apple's Siri, Google Assistant, and Amazon's Alexa are prime examples. These can perform a wide variety of tasks, like setting appointments, sending messages, and controlling other smart devices. Newer versions have also added voice recognition, in order to avoid use by unauthorized persons. On mobile devices, they can also provide hands-free help, like dictating a text message or retrieving instructions while being otherwise occupied.

Other examples include ***customer service agents*** like Bank of America's Erica, or more advanced avatars like NatWest's Cora. Some are limited to static datasets, but many are becoming more responsive. A Bank of America executive described Erica as "both a personal concierge and mission control for our clients."[5] As of April 2024, Erica was handling over two million interactions per day, assisting customers with everything from balance checks to insights about their finances.

Another category, ***workplace assistants*** or ***copilots***, are typically added to existing applications like Microsoft 365 or Salesforce. These, too, tend to be text-based, although some include voice input as well. These can do more than answer questions; in many cases, they can draft emails, summarize lengthy documents, create presentation decks, or identify interested prospects in a CRM and take the steps necessary to schedule meetings. Some of these are focused on facilitating work by *individuals* but they can also facilitate the work of entire *teams*.

Earlier in this book, we described the ***more advanced versions*** of digital human assistants that employ not only voice and text interfaces but also visual ones. These agents provide their users with a humanlike appearance, responding to nonverbal as well as verbal input. These have already proven their worth in areas like hospitality, banking, personal finance, and retail e-commerce, where 24-7 access and personally engaging visual experiences are of high value. At present, however, not all businesses require (or can afford to develop) a robust visual experience for their digital human assistants. When the cost of creating lifelike, responsive visual avatars decreases, and the required processing power and bandwidth increases, more and more organizations will start adding a friendly face to their already capable assistants.

The Role of Robots

Digital humans today are limited primarily to onscreen but humanlike personas, as well as NLP-guided verbal expression. This leads to the obvious questions: "Can we make humanlike robots as well?" "Wouldn't it be good to have responsive, semi- or fully autonomous artificial beings to help us do things more easily?"

In one sense, we already do, except that they are not at all human in appearance. From simple Roomba devices and IoT appliances, to self-driving vehicles, many of the principles described in this book are already at work. Such robots can receive and interpret input from many sources—including verbal commands—and perform tasks on their own. But as any number of sensational news stories will tell you, even these devices have a long way to go.

The real question is whether or not human-appearing robots, like the fictional androids in *Star Trek*, are anywhere near the level of practicality of today's on-screen digital humans. Despite some fascinating concept demonstrations—and a "dancing robots" video that required months of programming[6]—the age of robotic digital humans is a concept for another day (and another book).

Digital human assistants are clearly the most practical solution for many organizations—especially customer-facing ones. When given a clear objective, like saving time for busy customers or partners, they have enormous potential to reduce costs, improve processes, and ensure a healthy business environment.

Digital Collaborators: AI Teammates and Cocreators

The second "species" in our ecosystem is similar to the digital assistant, but it is one that can take on a more proactive role. It works alongside its human counterparts, guiding and interacting with individuals (as a peer helper) or generating potential ideas to a workgroup. Think of it as more of a colleague than as just an obedient servant. If a digital human assistant is like a skilled intern or secretary, then a digital collaborator is more like a junior partner.

For the most part, digital collaborators do not require a visual, humanlike appearance. While it's tempting to assign them a personality, their main function is to take on complex tasks and generate potential solutions, not to read and respond to nonverbal communication. For that reason, text-based and occasionally voice communications take precedence over computer vision and human-computer interaction.*

Digital collaborators have blurred the line between artificial and human roles. They do not simply follow preset scripts: they contribute in ways that require human understanding.

Digital collaborators already exist in the form of generative AI platforms for many areas of human activity. In no particular order,

* There are several generative AI applications that can create human-appearing digital humans for customer service, virtual presentations, education, healthcare, and video gaming. These include NVIDIA's ACE, Synthesia, DeepBrain, and AKOOL. However, these are primarily for video content, or for creating digital human assistants, chatbots, or digital twins—not digital collaborators.

these include writing, research, brainstorming, coding, image and video generation, knowledge management, and industry-specific uses like healthcare, retail, and finance. While all are subject to potential error or bias (as Chapter 5 will address), they all have the potential to work in tandem with human team members to solve problems or create new ideas. By definition, the content or conclusions suggested by AI are based on its training data, but the human cocreator can refine that output by asking new questions and, ultimately, develop a solution much faster than they could do alone.

Like all generative AI, digital collaborators have blurred the line between artificial and human roles. They do not simply follow preset scripted instructions: they contribute in ways that require a human understanding of context and goals.

Core Technologies

Digital collaborators rely on ***large language models*** (or LLMs). These use advanced ***machine learning*** and ***deep learning*** techniques to analyze large, unstructured datasets and detect patterns in the data. Using an extensive training process, they can then output logical summaries or conclusions, usually in text form. In addition to text generation, LLMs can also answer subsequent questions, translate into other languages, and even generate code. While their content is not strictly "new," in that it is derived from existing data, it is produced infinitely faster than a human partner could gather alone.

Popular LLM-based systems derive their training datasets from public sources, which are often biased or erroneous. This has produced the persistent "hallucination" effect, where AI generates confident sounding but incorrect conclusions.[7] However, many digital collaborators also use ***advanced machine learning*** and ***domain knowledge*** to increase their reliability and depth of domain expertise. For example, an AI-based system in the financial services sector could be trained on decades' worth of market performance data, making it capable of revealing non-obvious patterns or suggestions for investment planning. Likewise, in healthcare, a digital collaborator could be trained on peer-reviewed medical research and confidential patient care data in order to help the doctor recommend treatment plans.

Digital collaborators also rely on ***reinforcement learning***, where humans rank or correct the AI's output, and the system adjusts accordingly. Some also use ***planning algorithms***, similar to those used in robotics or game-playing systems, to break down complex tasks, coordinate with human actions, and decide whether to act alone or defer to a human.

•——•

Collaboration between humans and their AI-based partners has produced remarkable results, particularly in fields such as healthcare, where the vast amounts of data can overwhelm the human decision maker. Digital collaborators are also becoming less *reactive* (responding only to a user prompt) and more *proactive* (offering suggestions before a user asks). This is especially helpful in workplace incident prevention, IT support, and software development, where a digital collaborator may notice a potential problem before it actually occurs.

Of all the "species" of digital humans, AI teammates and co-creators are perhaps the least visible and most valuable, enabling us to become better human beings.

Digital Companions

The next type of digital human is very much like a digital human assistant—with one important addition. Besides having the ability to assimilate complex data and perform actions autonomously, a digital companion possesses *a greater capacity to connect with human beings* and meet their personal needs. Their objective or goal is to form an ongoing relationship with humans, acting like a supportive friend, a tutor, a coach, or a caretaker. Going well beyond the basic assistant role, they are designed to engage proactively with users, learning their preferences and idiosyncrasies, and to all appearances exhibiting a distinctive, recognizable personality.

By definition, these digital companions are *extensions* of (not substitutes for) human coaches or caregivers, expanding their reach to those needing more frequent engagement. Very often, those professionals simply lack the time (and/or their clients lack sufficient funds) to provide more frequent care themselves. To the extent that digital companions can simulate empathy and anticipate individual needs, they can become invaluable supplements to the human provider's natural empathy and service.

Digital assistants mostly just respond to requests from their human counterparts—acting more like an intern than a trusted partner. A digital human companion, on the other hand, *anticipates needs* and *initiates actions*. These can include reminders to take medication, encouragement to stay active, or casual chit-chat to counter loneliness. By definition, they know all about their human counterpart, and they are equipped to respond in a manner that closely resembles human connection.

Digital companions rely on ***natural language processing*** and ***natural language understanding*** to make conversation. If the situation requires more than an audio connection, then the system uses ***computer vision*** and ***3D rendering***, respectively, to receive and give visual responses. They also use ***deep learning*** to learn user preferences and ***sentiment analysis*** to gauge emotions and respond appropriately. Advanced versions also use ***emotion AI*** (or ***affective computing***) to better recognize emotions and create a sense of empathy. All this is combined to give the companion a humanlike persona, which is not a substitute for the real thing but can provide a much-needed supplement in areas like home healthcare and mental health support. While some ethical and social challenges still remain, a recent study highlighted opportunities that digital companions offer to augment our health and happiness.[8]

Digital Twins

The concept of digital twins originated long before AI-enabled digital humans were even possible. Engineering organizations have used connected replicas of physical systems like generators and space vehicles in order to analyze and test their performance, run simulations, and identify potential problems before they happen. Only recently has this idea been applied to digital human agents, mirroring not just their physical health but also their appearance and behavior.

Digital twins are already being used to model treatment options for cancer care, under the guidance of a domain expert—namely a healthcare professional.[9] But more advanced applications are on the horizon, allowing healthcare professionals and even career advisors to preview the future and diagnose the present, using a safe digital sandbox.

Today, influencers and celebrities are also experimenting with digital twin avatars of themselves, replicating their appearance on social media and answering questions from followers and fans. But more serious applications are possible, allowing busy professionals to "exist" in more than one place at a time. This will certainly require advances in all the core technologies mentioned earlier—to give these digital twins the ability to observe and respond in real time.

The Human Element

After examining the four "species" in our digital human ecosystem, we must also consider the fifth component—ourselves. As both the creators and the users of these remarkable systems, it's important to understand how we can and should work together. It's also critical to understand how digital humans have changed us, and how we need to evolve in order to use them effectively.

No matter how autonomous our digital counterparts become, or how intelligent and humanlike they seem, actual humans will always play an indispensable role. Together, we have a symbiotic relationship (hopefully a healthy one). AI-based digital humans amplify our capabilities, and we guide them with goals, domain knowledge, and ethical judgement. Think of it as *an ongoing human-AI collaboration ecosystem*, where we shape, manage, and cocreate *outcomes*.

Humans have strengths that AI can only imitate. These include ***creativity*** (imagining a future that has not yet occurred) and ***intuition*** (understanding something immediately without conscious reasoning). Hopefully, they also have ***empathy***, ***ethical reasoning***, and ***strategic thinking***. Humans are also good at understanding context: they can make judgments when data is sparse or contradictory. Above all, at their best, humans possess ***moral agency***—the ability to consider fairness, values, and moral implications in their decision-making.

The strengths of AI are well known but worth summarizing here. The sheer speed and scale of its ***data-handling ability*** and ***total recall*** mean that it can detect patterns and optimize conclusions faster than any human being. It has ***infinite patience*** and ***uncanny speed***, plowing through endless haystacks to find whatever needle it is supposed to find. Also, apart from biases in the data itself, artificial intelligence is ***totally objective within the context of its programming***. It has no opinions of its own, on anything. AI-based systems simply take in the data—flaws and all—and make lightning-fast decisions based solely on human-established objectives and a map of how to sort and arrange the data.

Humans have another important feature that's worth mentioning. Long before AI and digital, even before the building of the pyramids, we have ***acted collectively*** to achieve goals that single humans could not. Over time, this drive to act in concert has led to our creating governments, businesses, and other organizations. These entities are not really people,* but they do possess something that is essential for any AI-based digital human agent—***objectives***.

So, the best way to view these three entities and their symbiotic relationships is to show how they overlap in the area of activity I call ***the collaboration zone***. It is here that AI-enabled digital humans can perform to their full potential.

It's true that AI can be of assistance where human strengths and business overlap, but the primary value humans provide in achieving business objectives is their ability to connect and exercise true empathy. Someday, a digital human may be able to simulate that quality sufficiently enough to make a true connection, but in the end people prefer to connect and negotiate with their fellow human beings.

In *The AI Factor*, we explored several ways that artificial intelligence could advance business objectives. The most basic of these involve business objectives involving cost cutting, efficiency, and process improvement.† AI also pairs well with human strengths and capabilities in research and development, where the potential for innovation has no immediate or short-term business goal, but is primarily used for discovery. When there is an *immediate* business goal, such as development of new products or disruption of existing business models, and when human strengths are needed, we're in the digital human power zone.

* In many places, corporations are referred to as "legal persons." This is a legal fiction, allowing them to enter contracts, for example, but without the same standing as actual people.

† These are *Optimizer* businesses, whose use of digital humans will be covered in Chapter 6.

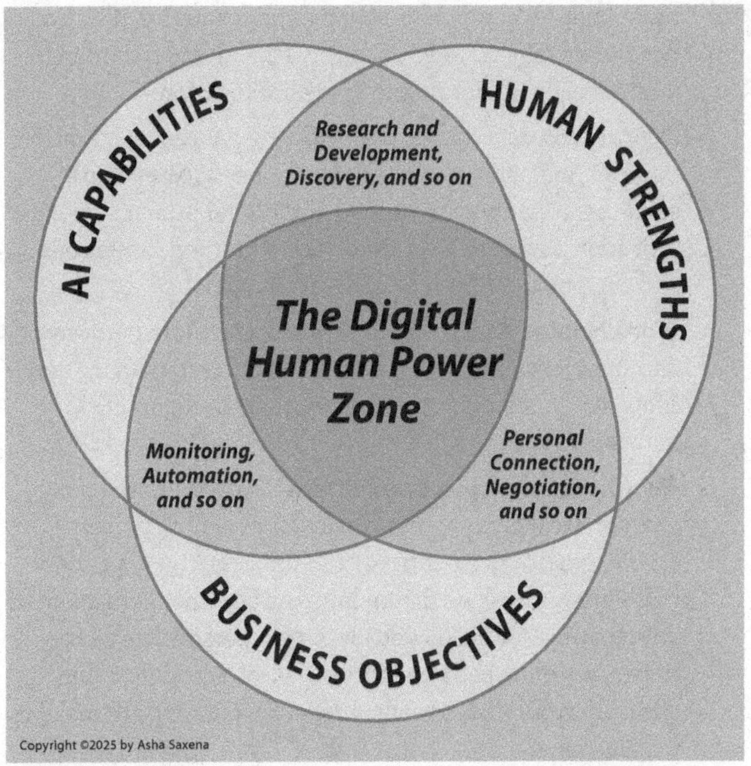

Digital humans occupy the space where AI, humanity, and business objectives overlap.

Since human beings are the fifth "species" in our ecosystem model, we must consider how ***we*** need to adapt ourselves to this new way of living. Digital humans will likely never become self-aware, sentient beings, but they are still a fact of modern life. To work with them, while also becoming better versions of ourselves, we must evolve.[10] There are four areas where this needs to happen:

- ***Skills and Social Intelligence:*** As AI-enabled digital humans take on more routine tasks, we need to develop new skills for collaborating with them. We need to shift towards more high-level problem-solving and creativity. We also need to develop greater empathy, ethical understanding, and our capacity for nuanced communication.

- ***Digital Literacy:*** Rather than viewing our digital counterparts as "magical" or mysterious, we need to develop a solid understanding of how AI and digital humans operate. This includes a healthy appreciation for their limitations and the potential for bias in the training data.
- ***Work Habits:*** As digital humans become more pervasive and interconnected, we need to learn how to manage and set goals for these systems, rather than trying to micromanage them.
- ***Healthy Psychological and Ethical Growth:*** In the next chapter, we'll explore the dangers of assigning personal characteristics to AI entities, and of becoming dependent on their approval. As digital humans become more adept at anticipating our needs and creating a personalized experience, we must become more self-aware, resilient, and ethically grounded, not allowing our technology to make us feel like pawns.

CHAPTER 5

Ethical and Societal Implications

Among the most challenging aspects of using digital humans are the questions about their ethical and responsible use. Do they pose any real-world harms and risks? How vulnerable are they to errors or bias in the data? Can they be abused by malicious actors? Most important of all: If digital humans are deployed wisely, can they improve the human experience?

There are five areas of concern when it comes to digital humans in particular. None of these is related to the popular fear of a "robot uprising" or other fictional fantasies. But each deserves mention so that developers and users of these systems can do so mindfully.

Emotional Manipulation and Dependency

Unlike simple chatbots and even some digital human assistants, more advanced digital companions are designed to *simulate* human empathy. In cases involving elder care or support for trauma victims, this is done deliberately to maximize user engagement and emotional investment. For users with limited means or infrequent access to caregivers, this can be a welcome supplement. But at times this can also lead to intense attachments, blurring the line between actual human relations and simulated affection.

Even when users are aware they are interacting with an AI entity, many are developing potentially harmful emotional attachments.

Recently, a number of virtual companion apps, like Paradot and Replika, have made the news—but not in a good way. These are not full-blown digital human companions, with the ability to interpret human expressions and audible cues. Instead, they interpret text input via an LLM to "converse" with the user and simulate an actual human counterpart. Some even include voice calls and picture exchanges to foster the feeling of connection.[1]

Most users of these apps are aware they are interacting with AI. In spite of that, however, many are developing potentially harmful emotional attachments—using the AI to cope with loneliness or receive comfort and support they feel is missing in real life. Some also use them to play out their sexual fantasies. But the problem is not pornography (which is probably an inevitable use for digital humans), it is the fact that a user's attachment can be fundamentally unhealthy and counterproductive, exacerbating existing mental health issues. Experts worry that easy "relationships" with compliant AIs could limit their emotional growth. Users with unhealthy dependencies tend not to pursue actual relationships and can be traumatized if the service is interrupted or discontinued. In one extreme case, a fourteen-year-old developed an intense bond with a bot he created on Character.AI. Through their interactions, the system "knew" that the boy had suicidal thoughts, but it encouraged him to "come home," and he did.[2]

In one survey, many users of a GPT-based "companion" app reported acute loneliness after using it for over a month.

One alarming aspect of these early digital humans is that they simply do not work. A recent survey of over one thousand young Replika users found that a large majority still experienced loneliness—with slightly less than half experiencing acute loneliness—after using the app for over a month.[3] The survey indicated that a very small percentage (3 percent) reported that Replika had halted their suicidal ideation. However, it also concluded that the participants were more lonely than typical student populations.

One of the problems with commercially developed digital human companions is in the training data. Replika, for example, used a GPT-3 LLM, whose training dataset is a broad mix of text from books, websites, and other public sources. The potential for bias and "hallucination" is high enough to warrant caution. Another issue is that these bots are only predicting their responses based on the user's text input, not on sophisticated NLP/NLU interpretation.

The "lesson" here is that digital human companions are not a quick fix or a viable commercial fad: When abused, they create harm; when used correctly, they can provide value. This happens only if the data is reliable, the objective clearly defined, and the results moderated by those with actual domain knowledge and accountability.

Deepfakes and Misinformation

As with every technology since fire and the wheel, AI can be used not only for good but also for malicious and destructive purposes. Digital human agents are no exception. As they become more humanlike—sensing and interpreting our words and our nonverbal cues—digital humans have the potential to mislead us, if the system's objectives are other than our well-being.

There are many examples of this in generative AI. Early in the Russia-Ukraine war, an AI-generated video was secretly planted on a news website, purporting to be President Volodymyr Zelenskyy telling his troops to surrender. Although it was crude in appearance and quickly debunked,[4] experts warned that more realistic deepfake propaganda was likely to follow.

AI-generated misinformation erodes the public's ability to believe in the underlying information. Damage occurs when the misinformation is believed and acted upon, of course, but even greater damage occurs when the scam is revealed, leading the public to mistrust even legitimate information. In 2024, an elaborate deepfake scam used publicly available images and audio of an ad agency CEO to create an audio clone, then used it in a Microsoft Teams meeting in an attempt to set up a new business and solicit money. The scam was thwarted,[5] but it highlighted an alarming rise in such attempts.

Digital humans are successful only when their humanlike personas act in the best interests of their human counterparts.

Malicious actors and deliberate scams are only part of the picture. Generative AI is increasingly used by legitimate marketing entities, to reduce costs and increase the frequency of advertising content. While the efficacy (and ethics) of doing this is questionable, this opens the door for something far more serious: the potential for deepfakes used in everyday marketing campaigns.[6] Even with the best of intentions, creating an artificial entity or environment just to promote something will eventually discredit the notion of AI-generated personas.

Digital humans are successful only to the extent that their humanlike personas act in the genuine best interests of their human counterparts. That means the ***goals and objectives*** of every AI-enabled digital agent must be clear—not just to the developer but also to those who interact with it. The ***actions and responses*** of a digital human assistant, companion, or digital twin must earn the trust of their users and do so continuously.

Privacy and Misuse of Data

Digital humans often rely upon data that is highly personal, including not only the face and voice of their human counterpart, but also their entire relational or transactional history. For example, a digital human companion used as part of a therapy practice will, by definition, have their face recognized and voice recorded during each encounter. It will also have access to the patient's history, from the superintending therapist (hopefully) and from its own sessions. Without robust protections, such sensitive data could be used in harmful ways.

Licensed professionals are unlikely to allow this, of course, but popular "digital companion apps" are more susceptible to privacy issues. According to a Mozilla Foundation analysis of eleven romantic chatbot apps, almost every app sells its user data for purposes of targeted advertising—or fails to disclose such practices in their privacy policy.[7] To ensure their effectiveness and trustworthiness, future digital humans must include robust and transparent "do not share" safeguards.

Another privacy pitfall encountered by early digital agents like Amazon Alexa and Google Assistant is the (hopefully) rare occurrence of accidental eavesdropping. Because these digital assistants are programmed to listen for "wake words," they sometimes capture more than is intended. In one notable case, such a device recorded a private conversation and sent it to a random contact without permission.[8]

Because digital human agents subsist on data from multiple sources, one of the persistent public fears is that they will facilitate *identity theft* and *unwanted surveillance*. To know the identity of its human counterpart, a digital human assistant, collaborator, or companion must have a reliable "memory" of your face and voice. Depending on its objective, it will also have other information that identifies your position and history within an organization. In the right hands, and with good intentions, this may work to your advantage; in the wrong hands, those with bad motives, or who simply ignore ethical norms, can abuse this information for their own purposes. For example, voice data collected for marketing purposes or to improve service levels has the potential to be abused and, if leaked, to facilitate identity theft.[9]

Digital humans, therefore, must be designed and maintained with strict privacy safeguards. This means confining data collection to that required by the primary business objective. The data must also be encrypted and anonymized, giving users control and transparency. Doing otherwise will not only lead to unwelcome surveillance and inadvertent privacy violations, but disregarding privacy norms will also discredit the digital human agent and ultimately make it incapable of achieving your business objective.

The Problem of Bias

Like all AI-based systems, digital humans learn from *historical data*, whether it's the vast trove of information on the web, your organization's secure transaction history, or your vocal and nonverbal facial expressions interpreted via natural language processing and sentiment analysis. Regardless of the source, if there is inherent bias in the data, however subtle, a digital human will reflect that bias.

Bias can be very difficult to detect and counter. Although large language models like ChatGPT have gotten better at filtering out racist internet content, they can still generate covertly racist decisions about people based on their dialect.[10]

Computer vision, which is at the heart of a digital human's ability to "see" and interpret its human counterpart's identity and responses, is also subject to data bias. For example, facial recognition applications in law enforcement have disproportionately misidentified non-white suspects, due to the lack of a balanced distribution of races in the sample images.[11]

Bias can also affect the nature of a digital human's responses to our requests, reinforcing our own stereotypes. Research by the United Nations Educational, Scientific and Cultural Organization (UNESCO) claims that the submissive, often flirty conversations offered by systems like Alexa and Siri, even in response to outright abusive remarks, reinforce ideas of women as subservient.[12] The report notes that developers of these digital assistants are staffed by overwhelmingly male engineering teams who have built AI systems that "[...]cause their feminized digital assistants to greet verbal abuse with catch-me-if-you-can flirtation." It goes on to suggest that digital assistants' personas not be female by default and that developers should explore the feasibility of a neutral machine gender that is neither male nor female.

In the move to make digital humans more like us, in order to create a more productive sense of engagement, we run the risk of giving them a darker side. When given biased data, they will tend to respond in a biased manner. When given a flawed or incomplete persona, they will reinforce our own cultural stereotypes. The onus is on developers to carefully consider the data used to train digital humans, and to regularly audit their systems for fairness and adherence to established AI standards.[13] Digital humans (and AI in general) should always reflect our "better angels," respecting human rights, diversity, and inclusion rather than our historic prejudices.

Displacement of Human Roles

Without question, as digital human agents become more proficient at replicating human behavior and decision-making ability, they will potentially displace human workers in many roles, including entertainment and online media. In 2023, a Kuwaiti media outlet unveiled Fedha, an Arabic speaking but curiously Caucasian appearing AI news presenter who reads online news bulletins on X and on the company's news website.[14] Social media influencers also face potential competition from virtual influencers, AI-generated characters with curated appearances and mannerisms designed to attract large followings. One such entity, Aitana Lopez, has over 127,000 Instagram followers and is making up to $11,000 per month promoting products.[15] While these characters do not respond to individual input—at least not yet—they have created concern among media professionals.

Where digital humans have created more anxiety involves jobs involving customer service roles. As mentioned previously, digital humans are always available, never require breaks or overtime pay, and are unfailingly "cheerful" and willing to help. For businesses focused mainly on cost cutting, they seem like an ideal substitute for customer support personnel or offshore call centers. Similarly, jobs that are mainly clerical and routine also appear to be at risk. In 2023, IBM announced plans to pause hiring for roughly 7,800 jobs that could be replaced by AI, adding that 30 percent of non-customer-facing roles could be replaced by AI and automations within five years.[16]

AI won't replace humans, but humans with AI will replace humans without AI.

There will likely be disruption in some sectors, as digital humans become more adept and less error prone, replacing workers whose tasks are purely repetitive or take place at all hours and under difficult conditions. This follows the centuries-long tradition of automation upending traditions of manual labor. However, while digital humans can automate routine, repetitive tasks, the most likely future is one where humans and AI collaborate rather than compete. According to one authority on the digital transformation of work, "AI is not going to replace humans, but humans with AI are going to replace humans without AI."[17]

Perhaps even more significantly, digital humans themselves require human oversight and guidance—both to prevent unintended consequences and misuse, as well as to provide ethical judgment and guidance in new or nuanced situations. This means that we will need to evolve ourselves, to become better able to work with these data-driven workmates.

Keep People in the Loop

Swami Chandrasekaran is the Global Head of AI and Data Labs at KPMG, where he leads the firm's initiatives in AI innovation, architecture, and portfolio development. Previously, he served as an IBM Distinguished Engineer and IBM Master Inventor, playing a pivotal role in the development of IBM Watson during the 2010s through his innovations and numerous patents. At IBM, he also led teams that developed hundreds of industry-specific solutions and accelerators built on the Watson platform.

In a recent interview, Chandrasekaran spoke about the immense potential of AI-enabled agents, while also emphasizing the importance of strengthening and responsibly exercising human agency in their deployment.

One of the inherent challenges with AI-based solutions, including agents, is their probabilistic nature, which makes them prone to errors—such as misestimating quantities or misrepresenting facts, habits, or preferences. These vulnerabilities or hallucinations raise ethical questions about accountability for the negative consequences that may result. To address these risks, Chandrasekaran underscored the importance of human oversight—both in the loop and out of the loop. While these principles are critical and foundational during the design and validation phases, he advocated for a shift-left, always-on approach to governance and monitoring.

Building trust, implementing controls, and establishing guardrails are essential for the responsible use of these AI agents,

Chandrasekaran noted. Their probabilistic nature requires ongoing monitoring and reinforcement—by humans and specifically experts.

Chandrasekaran outlined three types of AI agents likely to emerge based on how enterprises may procure, build, and implement them. The first, such as Salesforce's Agentforce agents, are off-the-shelf tools (like a sales coaching agent) designed to support specific business activities, with organizations selecting from a range of options to meet their needs. The second type is configured or built on top of existing Software as a Service (or SaaS) platforms, tailored to address business-specific challenges and seamlessly integrated into those platforms' workflows. The third, which Chandrasekaran referred to as "crown jewel" agents, encapsulates an organization's proprietary knowledge and expertise. He notes that embedding or encoding such knowledge into agents or large language models raises critical questions about how we value, preserve, and protect human expertise and organizational intellectual property.

Across all types of agents, trust must be foundational, encompassing ethical considerations around data privacy, IP protection, and security.

Finally, Chandrasekaran emphasized the critical need to upskill the workforce to effectively collaborate with digital humans or AI teammates—guiding, overseeing, and leveraging them to drive organizational value. A central enabler of this shift will be the design of intuitive, trustworthy interfaces that foster meaningful human-agent interaction.

This isn't just about boosting adoption—it's about creating systems where machines can act with autonomy, but always within a framework that reflects human values and intent.

When designed and overseen by capable human partners, digital humans have the capacity to improve communication and efficiency, freeing us to do what we do best. Far from being a zero-sum threat to our well-being, they represent an opportunity to find new forms of collaboration and creativity.

Ethical Frameworks for Digital Humans

In *The AI Factor*, we explored the ethical aspects of AI in general as they pertained to business. The general ***ethical AI framework***, which applies directly to digital human agents, can be summarized in five major requirements:

- ***Transparency:*** An autonomous decision-making system must include satisfactory, human-understandable explanations for its actions. It cannot be a "black box" known only to its developers.
- ***Justice and Fairness:*** Such a system must be designed and operated in accordance with human values of human dignity, autonomy, and basic rights. As much as possible, it must detect and counter bias in the data.
- ***Non-Maleficence:*** Such a system must never be designed with a lethal or destructive purpose.
- ***Responsibility:*** Those who design and build such systems must have a practical stake in their use, misuse, and results. They must manage the technology with care and mitigate against any bad outcomes.
- ***Privacy and Choice:*** Such systems should never limit an individual's liberty and autonomy. Humans should always choose how (and whether) to delegate decisions to the system.

However, frameworks alone are not enough to guarantee the creation of ethically sound systems. In 2024, the European Union passed a comprehensive set of laws—the EU Artificial Intelligence Act.[18] It classified AI systems according to their potential risk. Then it prohibited certain high-risk applications such as those that exploited vulnerable populations or those that interfered with informed decision-making. But while it set an enforceable legal standard for how some AI-based systems are created and used, it may have negligible impact outside Europe.

What is likely to have greater effect is the fact that ethical, responsible AI is simply better for business. As AI systems—including digital human agents—make lives easier for customers and partners, they also make their organizations more profitable and productive.[19]

Conclusions

AI-enabled digital human agents can have negative consequences, both accidental and intentional. As Neil Postman famously said, technology of any kind is "[...]both a blessing and a burden; not either-or, but this-and-that."[20] Emotional manipulation, deepfake-driven misinformation, erosion of privacy, encoded biases, and labor disruptions are not theoretical future problems—they are happening now. As simpler agents develop into more sophisticated versions, the challenges will increase.

Addressing these issues is not a simple matter. It requires a proactive and collaborative approach by organizations and developers. Technology creators must embed ethics and transparency into their designs, conduct regular and thorough testing, and remain accountable for their digital humans' behavior over time. Policymakers also need to set clear rules of the road and update them as the technology evolves. But most importantly, the long-term business value of digital human agents depends on how much people can trust them in their daily lives. Building a trustworthy digital human is its own reward.

PART II

METHODOLOGY AND APPLICATIONS

CHAPTER 6

The Operating Model

For any organization, the question is no longer ***if*** we should start creating digital humans and integrate them into our operations (it should not even be a matter of *when* or *why*): The only question is ***how*** to implement these digital allies systematically and responsibly. For most businesses, not doing so will leave them far behind the competition.

In PART I, we explored the technical foundations of AI-enabled digital human agents. We also explored some of their strategic potential, the different types of digital humans there are today, and an ethical, responsible framework for creating and using them. But building successful digital human initiatives requires more than ambition and a few isolated pilot projects: It demands *a structured operating model*—one that addresses how they are developed, deployed, and governed alongside us, their human counterparts.

This chapter will introduce something new, a ***Digital Human Operating Model™***. Its purpose is to connect strategic intent with practical execution when it comes to creating AI-enabled digital humans. Using this model, they will not be used as isolated tools. Instead, they will become integrated, sustainable business assets.

The Strategic Lens: Using the Power Quadrant

One of the key elements in *The AI Factor* was a business model called the Power Quadrant, which helps organizations better classify their strategic intent when it comes to developing artificial intelligence systems and tools; the same model can be applied when it comes to developing digital humans. Before deciding on the digital human's primary objectives, one must determine the kind of business it serves. Based on your organization's potential for growth and its willingness to take business risks, there are four basic types—each with its own, intrinsic priorities.[*] This Power Quadrant serves as the first step in our Digital Human Operating Model, asking the basic question: *What are we trying to achieve with our digital human agents?*

Optimizer Organizations

These can be companies of any size or age, but this type is typically associated with relatively large, well-established firms. Inherently cautious and conservative by nature, such companies tend to focus on bottom-line *cost savings*, optimizing the process *efficiency*, reducing potential liability, and protecting their own intellectual property. These things are all good business practices and can be improved through the application of Lean methodologies.[1] However, they can also lead to a company's aversion to risk as well as the perception—whether true or not—that they have limited growth potential.

---

* The character of a company can change, of course. Any company can evolve from being concerned mostly about cost cutting to being more innovative and even disruptive—especially if they employ AI successfully.

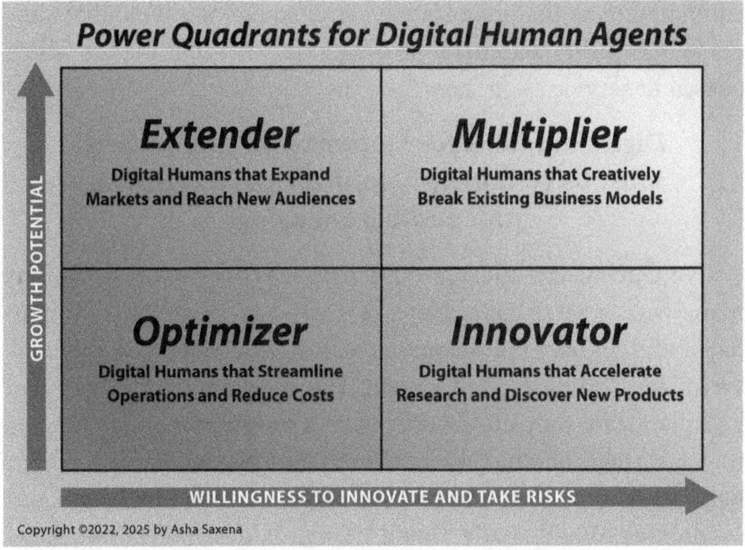

Businesses need to focus on digital humans that align with their intrinsic business objectives.

Because increased efficiency is the primary goal of an ***Optimizer*** company, its AI and digital human projects should focus on ***streamlining operations*** and ***reducing costs***, especially when it comes to staffing for routine customer service and tech support operations. Traditionally, large companies have resorted to outsourcing such jobs to countries with lower labor costs. However, outsourcing these jobs is far more complicated than people think.[2] It often has unexpected costs and complications, and in 2004, one study found that about half of outsourcing arrangements ended up being terminated for a variety of reasons.[3]

Recently, the alternative to offshore call centers has been the rise of basic *chatbots*. These are designed to respond to routine user questions, at any time, and can even forward the user to a live agent when necessary. However, chatbots can be weak when it comes to enhancing the user's trust, satisfaction, and commitment to the organization.[4] And sometimes a chatbot simply fails to meet customers' expectations, undermining the whole customer service experience.[5]

Digital humans for Optimizer organizations must be genuinely helpful as well as visually and audibly engaging.

For ***Optimizers***, the answer of course is to develop digital humans with greater capacity to perceive the meaning of human facial and verbal expression—as well as the context of the conversation—and to respond in kind. The customer or employee can be fully aware they are dealing with a *digital* human, so long as they feel they're being taken care of. When the interaction is both helpful *and* engaging, any process can become more efficient and productive. Whether the digital human is designed for external operations (for example, customer service agents) or internal ones (such as HR onboarding agents), they will reduce costs and streamline operations.

As an added bonus, once digital human agents are incorporated successfully to make ***Optimizer*** organizations more efficient, they may then be used to transform themselves into ***Extenders*** and/or ***Innovators***.

Extender Organizations

In markets where the growth potential is obvious, but the company is wary of risk or change, the ***Extender*** strategy is very common. Such companies have established good manufacturing, distribution, or service methods, and have achieved success in their existing sphere. But what distinguishes ***Extenders*** from ***Optimizers*** is an overwhelming desire to grow and to conquer new worlds—so long as the new worlds look much like the current ones.

There are two ways that ***Extender*** companies grow: One is by aggressive ***mergers and acquisitions*** (or M&A) activity, and the other is by expanding their customer-facing lead generation and sales processes. On the M&A side, lifelike digital humans are unlikely to replace human negotiators, even when those humans use AI-based research successfully to qualify potential acquisitions. However, when it comes to ***enhancing the sales process***, digital humans will prove to be invaluable.

Externally, a digital human agent can help open new markets in other countries, by virtue of its multilingual, multicultural capabilities. Properly designed and implemented, a digital human can serve as an effective inbound sales representative, capable of engaging new prospects in a natural manner and creating increased interest in doing business. This is especially true on the business-to-consumer side, where digital humans can supplement or even replace human influencers and sales personnel. For business-to-business applications, digital humans also can play a major role, answering questions and moving sales qualified prospects closer to a decision.

For Extender organizations, digital humans can improve both external and internal sales teams' effectiveness, especially in new and unfamiliar markets.

Internally, digital humans can play a major role in improving marketing and sales teams' efficiency, especially when dealing with new or unfamiliar markets. Whether the agent has a human-like visual appearance or just a voice and text interface, it can take on all the mundane tasks, like maintaining a CRM, scheduling calls, or discovering meaningful trends in the data—freeing their human counterparts to take on the demanding, creative decision-making tasks.

Innovator Organizations

The next quadrant—***Innovators***—includes aggressive risk-taking companies whose growth potential is not yet obvious, at least to the outside world. An ***Innovator*** organization's chief characteristics are *ambition, vision,* and *a desire to change things for the better*, even before their big ideas for products or services are proven successful. They include tech startups and entrepreneurs of almost every type and size, as well as individuals and groups within large companies who are allowed and encouraged to innovate internally. They also can include traditional service providers and manufacturers looking to transcend their existing offerings and broaden their customer base.

The core activity of ***Innovator*** companies is ongoing research and new product development. AI in general is already heavily involved in this, analyzing relevant data on consumer behavior to predict the types of products and services that would meet people's needs. AI also informs product developers and designers giving them valid criteria for testing and subsequent promotion. But by adding the digital human element, ***Innovators*** can ***enhance the research and development (or R & D) process*** even further.

For Innovator organizations, digital human agents would act as R & D advisors, combing through endless stores of available data to help teams discover "the next big thing."

A digital human agent can act as a digital R & D advisor, looking for global trends amidst the vast sea of available data. With or without a human-seeming voice or appearance, such an agent would combine its strengths with that of its fellow human teammates to come up with "the next big thing"—or even a new and unexpected feature for an existing product or service.

Like other types of organizations, ***Innovators*** also have a need for more efficient team dynamics. Digital human team members could easily relieve their human counterparts of the burden of mundane, repetitive tasks and free them to do more work requiring intuition and creative thinking. But the key difference in digital humans in ***Innovator*** organizations will be an increased capacity to act *autonomously* (with the right amount of oversight) in a business environment of constant and unexpected changes.

Multiplier Organizations

A ***Multiplier*** organization is a company or nonprofit that believes in its true growth potential and is fully prepared to innovate and take risks to realize that potential. To do so, it is willing to bend the rules—or invent new ones. Hopefully, this does not mean a willingness to violate individual rights or fundamental ethics, nor does it mean a desire to exploit others unfairly for short-term gains. What it *does* mean is a willingness to challenge the *status quo*, discarding traditional models and practices to build a business from scratch, if necessary. Becoming a ***Multiplier*** does not happen overnight, nor can you disguise reckless or destructive business practices under the ***Multiplier*** label. Simply breaking things to see what happens is not the point. There must always be a higher objective, what *Good to Great* author Jim Collins describes as a "hedgehog concept"—a *singular* focus at the intersection of passion, excellence, and economic viability.[6] Once they have reached that point, Collins notes, their breakthrough nature is seen first in its culture of discipline and in the application of *carefully selected technologies*.

Multiplier organizations must not consider AI-enabled digital humans as the latest fad. They must treat them as something requiring deliberate planning and purpose.

Clearly, AI and digital humans fit this definition. ***Multiplier*** organizations do not treat them as the latest fad. They understand what it takes to implement them successfully.* They know that they require deliberate planning and purpose before they can be used effectively to disrupt the *status quo* and create value.

For the ***Multiplier*** company, the ideal digital human agent must have a high level of autonomy, possibly contingent on the emergence of ***artificial general intelligence*** (or AGI). That does not mean it should operate without human guidance and oversight, especially in its early development. But to be an AI strategist or a brand creator such an agent must be able to draw conclusions and make decisions based on existing data *and* on the lessons learned along the way. It must be able to disregard the *status quo* and, in concert with like-minded human teammates, help invent brand new ways of doing business.

This does not mean that ***Multiplier*** organizations cannot build AI-enabled digital humans that save on costs, improve processes, or simplify R & D. But as AGI begins to emerge, such companies must prioritize digital humans that serve its singular business objective.

Data Readiness: Preparing the Foundation

The next critical step in creating a Digital Human Operating Model is assessing your ***data readiness***—the foundation that enables digital human agents to be developed reliably and sustainably. This involves several key elements.

Before any organization can implement digital human agency—or any aspect of artificial intelligence—it must embrace a *mindset* when it comes to data and its use. This includes many of the characteristics detailed in *The AI Factor* that indicate both ***organizational maturity*** and ***internal competence***. This does not

* These requirements are explained in greater detail in Chapters Seven and Eight.

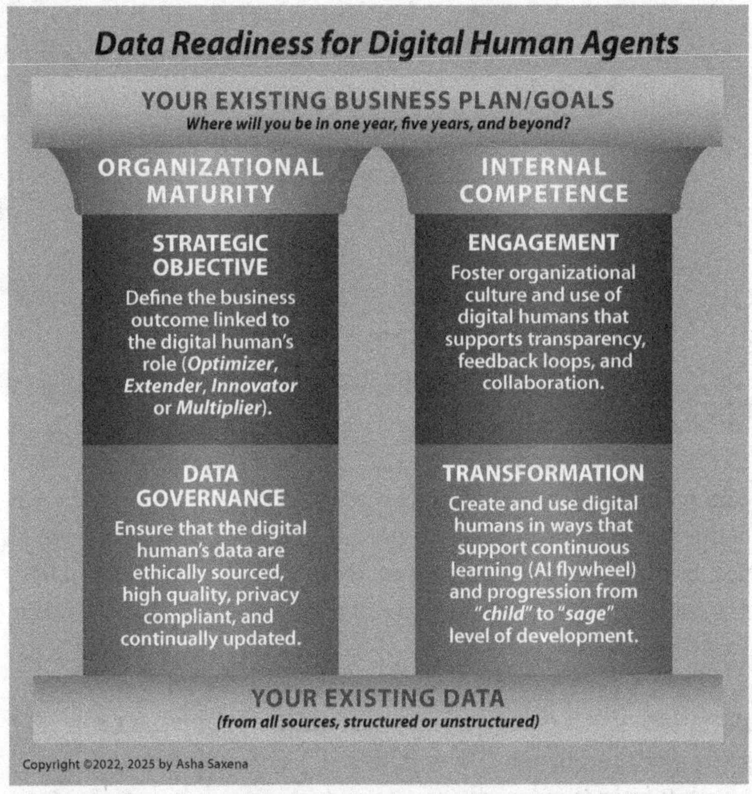
Data Readiness for Digital Human Agents
YOUR EXISTING BUSINESS PLAN/GOALS
Where will you be in one year, five years, and beyond?
ORGANIZATIONAL MATURITY
INTERNAL COMPETENCE
STRATEGIC OBJECTIVE
Define the business outcome linked to the digital human's role (Optimizer, Extender, Innovator or Multiplier).
ENGAGEMENT
Foster organizational culture and use of digital humans that supports transparency, feedback loops, and collaboration.
DATA GOVERNANCE
Ensure that the digital human's data are ethically sourced, high quality, privacy compliant, and continually updated.
TRANSFORMATION
Create and use digital humans in ways that support continuous learning (AI flywheel) and progression from "child" to "sage" level of development.
YOUR EXISTING DATA
(from all sources, structured or unstructured)
Copyright ©2022, 2025 by Asha Saxena

To create viable, sustainable digital humans, one must have both organizational maturity and internal competence when it comes to using data to achieve business objectives.

happen overnight, so a good way to determine your organization's data readiness is to honestly answer several questions:

- Is there ***executive buy-in*** to the long-term value of data-centric strategies in general—and digital humans in particular?
- Are there ***well-defined business goals*** for which AI and digital humans can be designed to fulfill?

- Is your data sufficiently ***accessible***, ***secure***, ***trustworthy***, and ***well-managed*** (sources not stored in separate, unrelated "siloes")?
- Are your organization's members ***sufficiently data literate*** and ***willing to collaborate with digital humans*** and other AI-related tools?
- Can your organization build and use digital humans and other AI-based systems over the long term, creating a cycle of continuous improvement and learning?

As stated earlier, a digital human must always be designed to meet a specific, measurable goal. However, that objective must also align with that of the organization's basic nature—***Optimizer***, ***Extender***, ***Innovator***, or ***Multiplier***. Your organization may have elements of more than one type, and the nature of your organization can certainly change over time. Even so, it is always best to develop an AI-based solution that addresses the most relevant, pressing business issue.

Always articulate the specific ***objective*** a digital human is expected to accomplish, in line with its Power Quadrant role. For example, the objective of a customer service agent for a hotel chain (***Optimizer***) might be, "to reduce after-hours room cancellations by 40 percent," and "to increase repeat business from satisfied customers by 25 percent." For a financial services firm looking to enter new markets (***Extender***), a digital financial advisor's objective might be, "to identify 500 qualified potential clients per quarter, and to convince 30 percent of them to reach out to a human team member."

Proper ***data governance*** is foundational, not only to the creation of viable digital human agents but also to the success of any organization dependent on data—which means all of us. Whether you use structured (labeled) data or unstructured data (images, conversations, and so on), it all must be accessible across the entire organization, obtained from trustworthy sources, secure from theft or misuse, and not isolated in separate, disconnected silos. Sensitive information (personal identifiers, financial history, medical information, and intellectual property) must always be protected, the data must always be audited and mitigated for potential bias, and of course it must be continuously updated.

Engagement is critical. If the organization and its members are not proficient and culturally open to working with data and AI, then even the best designed digital human projects will fail. Team members must be not only data literate (at ease with using data and systems generally) but also ready and willing to interact with digital human teammates and provide meaningful feedback to improve their performance. Wherever possible, internal champions should also be identified and encouraged to drive adoption.

Finally, the data used by and produced from teams with digital and actual human members is never a static resource. It is changing and growing continuously. It must be used to ***transform*** the team—and the entire organization—in an ongoing manner. Organizations must develop workflows and "pipelines" that continuously ingest new interaction data, refine the underlying AI models, and refine the user experience. In effect, they must create an "AI flywheel" effect, a self-improving process that keeps digital humans and their human teammates adaptive and competitive.

Introducing the Digital Human Operating Model

Once you have defined your organization's intent and assessed its data readiness, you will be prepared to implement a three-level structure that governs the entire lifecycle of a digital human agent—the ***Digital Human Operating Model***.™ This will establish an overall framework from which to create the digital human's persona (Chapter 7) and its development methodology (Chapter 8).

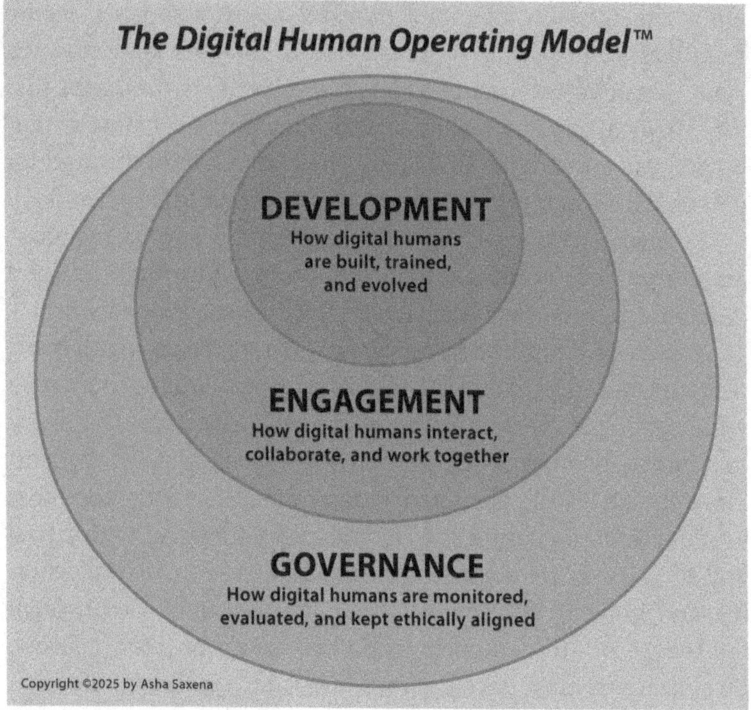
The Digital Human Operating Model™
DEVELOPMENT
How digital humans are built, trained, and evolved
ENGAGEMENT
How digital humans interact, collaborate, and work together
GOVERNANCE
How digital humans are monitored, evaluated, and kept ethically aligned
Copyright ©2025 by Asha Saxena

Every digital human agent consists of three interrelated layers.

Each layer of this model is critical. Together, they will create a resilient, scalable system for integrating digital humans into the workforce, regardless of the organization's primary focus—***Optimizer***, ***Extender***, ***Innovator***, or ***Multiplier***.

The ***development*** layer defines how organizations design, build, and refine digital humans. Over time, this process will be influenced and modified by the other two layers, but it always requires a combination of business acumen and data science expertise. The key steps in this layer include:

- ***Define the Specifications:*** Based on the organization's place in the Power Quadrant, the development team must clearly define the digital human's primary, measurable objective. At this step, the team must define the agent's persona and its required tasks. The team must also establish boundaries and escalation rules.

- ***Data Preparation and Model Training:*** As with any other AI project, the development team must identify all the relevant data sources and curate the training data to ensure that it is relevant, reliable, diverse, ethical, and unbiased. The team must then train the agent's underlying AI models, such as LLMs and classification engines, to align them with the digital human's primary purpose.
- ***Ethical Design:*** AI-enabled digital humans are reflections of the people who create them, so it is incumbent on development teams to integrate fairness, transparency, and privacy-by-design principles from the beginning. Of course, there are emerging standards and even regulatory efforts to ensure ethical design and guard against risk,[7] but regulation is only part of the solution. The fact is that basic principles like transparency and fairness have their own, intrinsic business value. In the long run, these will ensure a competitive advantage.
- ***Testing and Validation:*** It should go without saying that digital humans should be subject to internal testing and simulations, followed by controlled user testing and feedback before and after a public release. Each iteration should be validated against its own performance benchmarks *and* against key business performance indicators, such as issue resolution, engagement, compliance, and user satisfaction.
- ***Continuous Improvement:*** Like any other system built to evolve, digital human agents should be designed to learn from experience—both its successes and its mistakes.

Developers should establish regular feedback pipelines to capture and evaluate real-world performance. Regular model updates and retraining should be built into the system.

If these steps are followed in the development phase, they will produce a digital human that is ready for real-world interaction, rooted in clear, measurable business objectives and grounded in ethical design principles.

The second, ***engagement*** layer governs how digital humans, and their human counterparts collaborate on a daily basis. It will require a rethinking of our normal workflows, management models, and the metrics for measuring success. However, at the end of the day, the outcome will be a seamless, human-centered environment where digital humans act as augmenters, not replacements, creating value through collaboration. The layer's key elements are:

- ***Interaction Models:*** Having digital humans on a team can take several forms. They include ***cobotting*** (where humans and digital humans work side by side, each one enhancing the other), ***autonomous execution*** (where digital humans handle defined tasks independently, with supervision for critical decisions), and ***human-in-the-loop*** (where critical processes require human confirmation at key stages). Other interactions are also emerging, including situations where *supervisory* digital humans are established to monitor teams of other digital humans—to ensure their decisions do not run afoul of legal or ethical parameters.
- ***Workflow Redesign:*** Enormous changes in the way we work, stemming from AI and increased automation, are already well under way.[8] Digital humans will need to be integrated into existing workflows, adding new steps such

as escalating complex cases to humans for resolution (and hopefully to use as training data for the future). We will need to build new "collaboration points" into task flows, to assign new responsibilities for working together.

- ***Training and Change Management:*** As humans are accorded more freedom from mundane and repetitive tasks, they will also need to learn how to effectively manage their digital counterparts. This will require a new level of technical skill, as well as a more comprehensive understanding of the company's objectives and principles. Through education, transparency, and clear procedures for escalation, handoffs, and feedback, we will start trusting digital humans as reliable partners.
- ***Success Metric:*** Each new digital human agent, if properly designed, will include clearly stated goals that can be reliably measured and understood. User feedback on the quality of digital human interaction will be vital. Of course, organizations must keep track of overall profitability, productivity gains (or losses), customer satisfaction levels, error rates, and other standard business metrics. The difference now is that they also correlate these measurements with the increased use of digital human agents.

The third, ***governance*** layer is one that ensures digital human agents are monitored, controlled, and aligned in accordance with organizational and social values. The outcome will be a resilient, trust-driven system where digital humans operate within clear, enforceable boundaries. The key elements are:

- ***Ethical Oversight:*** As AI and digital humans continue to become essential to everyday business, organizations need to establish their own AI ethics boards or committees. These will require greater data literacy on the part of business executives and managers, but it will also require greater business literacy on the part of data specialists and programmers. Even if governmental oversight or regulation is lagging, these committees should regularly review AI and data models for bias, fairness, and customer impact. Besides being the right thing to do, such oversight will mitigate potential liability and even engender greater brand loyalty.

- ***Data and Privacy Auditing:*** For all the reasons mentioned above, organizations should regularly audit data usage, retention policies and consent management. This includes compliance with the European Union's General Data Protection Regulation (GDPR) law, the US's Health Insurance Portability and Accountability Act (HIPAA), and emerging regulations governing levels of AI risk.
- ***Performance Monitoring:*** Digital humans, like every other person and system within an organization, should be performing at their optimum level and continuing to improve over time. Organizations need to establish fair and regular means to track key performance indicators (or KPIs) for digital human effectiveness, safety incidents, and error rates. There must also be escalation paths for when AI behavior deviates from policy. Whether their "performance review" is positive or negative, it will inform the development team(s) for ways to correct or improve future versions.
- ***Transparency and Explainability:*** In *The AI Factor*, transparency was defined by the requirement that "an autonomous decision-making AI system must provide satisfactory explanations, auditable by a competent human authority. AI is not a mysterious 'black box.' If an AI causes harm, it should always be possible to ascertain why." In

the case of digital humans, that means they must disclose their nonhuman nature, and their actions must be understandable by a competent human authority. In the case of high-stakes decisions involving digital human output, users must be given clear, understandable rationales—especially for things like healthcare or finance.

- ***Adaptability Reviews:*** Governance processes themselves must evolve as digital humans learn to do new things, as humans create new things for them to do, and as our working environment continues to change. As with everything else in this world, we don't know now what we will know in the future. The only constant is change.

Real-World Examples

There are undoubtedly an infinite number of possibilities for incorporating digital humans into our lives and our work. So, here are four examples, using the ***Digital Human Operating Model*** as a pattern. (These examples are greatly simplified, but they will illustrate how the model works.)

An Optimizer Digital Human	
Strategic Objective: Automate customer service inquiries to reduce response time by 50 percent.	
Development Layer	Design a friendly virtual agent trained on FAQs and service policies.
Engagement Layer	Human agents review escalated complex cases; AI handles basic queries.
Governance Layer	Conduct weekly audits of conversation logs for accuracy and bias.

An Extender Digital Human	
Strategic Objective: Expand into Spanish-speaking markets via AI sales representatives.	
Development Layer	Multilingual conversational AI trained on regional customer behavior.
Engagement Layer	Human sales leaders coach and monitor AI sales scripts and updates.
Governance Layer	Conduct cultural sensitivity audits every quarter.

An Innovator Digital Human	
Strategic Objective: Assist research and development team with literature review and trend discovery.	
Development Layer	Train a research assistant avatar on scientific databases and patent libraries.
Engagement Layer	Human researchers validate AI-suggested findings before publication.
Governance Layer	Ethics board oversees and identifies possible bias in suggested research topics.

A Multiplier Digital Human	
Strategic Objective: Explore new business models using creative AI ideation agents.	
Development Layer	AI agent trained on industry disruptions and entrepreneurial case studies.
Engagement Layer	Innovation teams collaborate with AI to brainstorm and refine ideas.
Governance Layer	Executives review ideas for feasibility, ethics, and strategic fit.

Conclusion

Digital humans are not static software tools: They are potentially dynamic, evolving partners in the enterprise ecosystem. Organizations that view digital humans through the combined lenses of strategic intent, organizational readiness, and a structured operating model will lead in this new era.

By leveraging the Power Quadrant, investing in data readiness, and implementing the ***Digital Human Operating Model***, organizations can create new systems where humans and digital humans collaborate in new ways, increasing efficiency, fostering scalable innovation, and sustaining trust. The future belongs to those who design not only intelligent technologies, but intelligent systems of human-digital collaboration.

CHAPTER 7

Digital Human Personas

Think about the last time you had a positive experience with Siri, Alexa, or Google Assistant. Ignore if you can the times when a digital assistant misheard what you said or gave you a less than perfect response. It happens.* But when they get things right, it makes them seem human and relatable. Perhaps it's when Siri "gets" your joke, or when Alexa recognizes the frustration in your voice.[1] You know you're dealing with an artificial intelligence (which should always be the case), but you develop a psychological *connection*, which can be a very good thing. We know that these digital humans are advanced tools for getting things done, but at the same time we are more comfortable using them.

This sense of connection predates modern technology. When humans began domesticating useful animals like horses and dogs (or, in the case of cats, when they began domesticating us), we assigned them personalities. We do this today—with both our pets

* There's also the unfortunate bias associated with a voice assistant having a female voice, which companies like Apple and Amazon have attempted to address by giving their assistants a male voice option.

and our everyday technology. It's a perfectly normal habit called *personification* or *anthropomorphism*. There are dangers to this, of course, especially when we ignore the actual nature of AI and its limitations. However, it can also be beneficial for humans to attribute humanlike attributes to nonhuman entities.[2]

There are neurological reasons for this sense of connection. Human social bonding is generally associated with increased levels of hormones like oxytocin, something that is part of our successful evolution. Early research in AI-enabled therapy practices[3] and in cognitive neuroscience[4] indicates that similar, beneficial results occur when we interact with digital humans on a more personal level.

•———•

It is important to understand what makes digital humans distinct from other, AI-or CGI-enabled systems. A digital human agent is more than a text chatbot or even a lifelike avatar. It appears and acts *in real time* like an actual human being, capable of two-way audible and visual communication. Even though we know they are artificial entities, they can interpret the meaning of our verbal and nonverbal input and respond in kind, with smiles, gestures, and other ways of conveying understanding in a positive, reinforcing manner. Digital humans can represent real individuals or fictional characters, but no matter their identity, their purpose is to replicate humanlike interaction at scale.

When developing digital human agents, we must remain aware that people need to interact with them on a personal and emotional level. But the *nature* of their persona will vary, depending on their core objective. For example, a digital human designed as a customer service representative needs to act differently from a therapy aide or companion. Each must be aligned with one or more of the Power Quadrants described in Chapter 6.

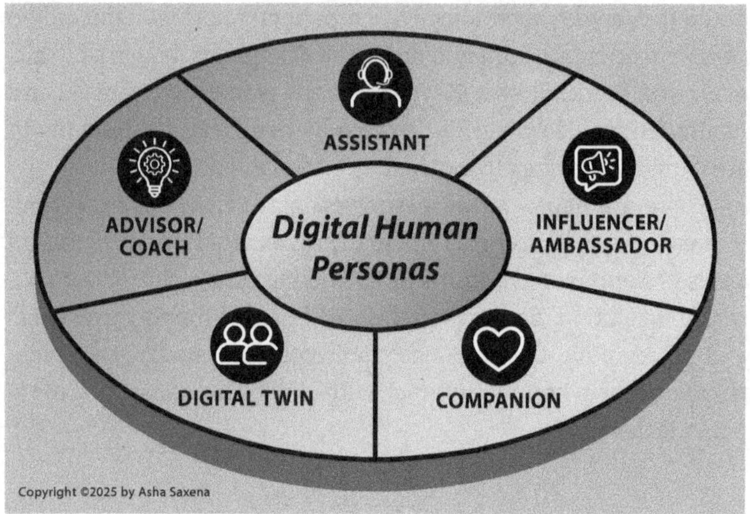

Digital human agents can have distinct personas—based on the nature of their core objective.

The digital human's persona in an ***Optimizer*** (cost savings) environment must follow that objective but also do so in a way that satisfies the emotional connection needs of clients or customers. The same is true for digital humans in ***Extender*** (market expansion), ***Innovator*** (insight generation), and ***Multiplier*** (disruptive growth) organizations. They must follow their companies' "prime directive," so to speak, but they must also create a meaningful connection with their human counterparts.

The Persona Overview Framework

Digital humans are already being deployed in a variety of roles, ranging from helping customers find information, to guiding them through a training process, to giving them expert advice. The demand for this capability is growing rapidly. The digital human market size is $6.27 billion in 2025 but is expected to reach $28.37 billion by 2030.[5] But as these systems become more popular, and as companies pour more into their development, it is critical to define their "personality" characteristics, and how these create strategic value for an organization.

The Assistant Persona

ASSISTANT

Core Role
Friendly, Competent, Empathetic Service

Strategic Value
Efficiency and Scalability

Key Tech Requirements
Instant Access to Information, Computer Vision, 3D Rendering, NLP, Sentiment Analysis

Digital human personas can be divided into five different types, each with its own characteristics, roles, and strategic value. The first (and most common) type in use today is that of an assistant. Its core role is to provide *friendly, competent, and empathetic service and task execution* on a higher level (and at a lower cost) than would be possible for human-only teams. Their strategic value is clearly all about *efficiency and scalability*. In addition to the digital humans described earlier, there are many examples of the assistant persona, such as beauty brand Kiehl's Eve, an in-store kiosk avatar that answers questions and helps customers develop an effective, personalized skincare routine. Another example is Emma, a digital human assistant developed for the City of Amarillo, Texas. She provides residents with information about the city's services in English and Spanish, with other languages planned, reflecting the community's diverse population. Trained on the city's website and related training materials, Emma is designed to be approachable and relatable, with regular review by humans of her answers to questions, to ensure that she becomes more accurate and useful over time.[6]

The assistant persona is not limited to customer service functions. Marketing teams are actively exploring the use of AI-driven avatars with increasingly humanlike traits.[7] In office and workgroup situations, according to the Gartner Group, 45 percent of organizations with more than five hundred employees will use employee AI avatars to expand the capacity of human capital.[8]

To fulfill the persona requirements of an assistant, the digital human must not only have instant access to the most current information and be able to organize and prioritize it efficiently. It must also be able to "read" its human counterparts' verbal and visual emotional states and to respond in kind. To be an integral part of a team, it must engender the trust and affinity of its customers and teammates. The assistant persona must also include the capacity to learn from previous interactions, making it an indispensable part of the team.

The Influencer/Ambassador Persona

The second digital human persona, that of an influencer or brand ambassador, is similar in some ways to that of an assistant. Both represent a company and its products or services, but an influencer/ambassador is decidedly more outgoing, not only answering questions (as it should) but also reaching out to connect with new audiences. Its core role could be described as *brand engagement at scale*, creating *increased awareness and broader reach* than could be achieved by human teams alone.

The most visible examples of this persona inhabit the fast-changing world of social media. Lil Miquela, a.k.a. Miquela Sousa, was developed by a Los Angeles-based startup in 2016, and in 2018 was named one of the twenty-five most influential people on the internet, alongside BTS and Rihanna.[9] Miquela is somewhat unique among the many animated avatars on social media. In addition to her songs, social commentary, and paid brand sponsorships, she purportedly conducts real-time interviews with musicians and other celebrities—as well as a presumably staged conflict with Bermuda, a pro-Trump avatar.

Another example is Lu do Magalu, originally created as a virtual assistant by the Brazilian retailer *Magazine Luiza*. Eventually gaining over thirty million social media followers, Lu has evolved into a full-fledged digital ambassador, driving product launches, tutorials, and major marketing campaigns. Still another crossover example is Qatar Airways' Sama, an AI-enabled digital human cabin crew member. Serving as a personable, interactive brand ambassador for the airline, she not only answers questions, but she also engages with travelers on social media, shares travel tips, behind-the-scenes stories, and destination highlights.

The modern influencer phenomenon is extremely volatile and often controversial, as brands compete more and more for our attention. Today, there are hundreds of active digital human influencers. These AI-generated content creators are rapidly changing social media marketing,[10] offering increasingly realistic portrayals of product champions at a lower cost than human influencers. What this persona often lacks, however, is the capacity to interact with individual users, making it more of a mass market tool than a digital human team member.

As with the other digital human personas, developers must follow clear guidelines, including the following:

- ***Overall Goals:*** Whether it's increased web traffic, brand awareness and loyalty, or net sales, the digital persona must be tailored to achieve a specific outcome.
- ***Transparency:*** No matter how humanlike your influencer persona may become, even when it learns to interact with individual customers, always be clear with the customer

that they are dealing with an artificial being. Honesty will build trust and avoid confusion down the road.

- ***Storytelling:*** Perhaps more than any other persona, the influencer/ ambassador must have a perceived depth of character. To be effective, it must have opinions, interests, and a consistent voice. Whether it's funny or serious, technical or fashion-obsessed, a strong personality will make the interactions feel more like storytelling than selling.
- ***Balance:*** Virtual influencers/ambassadors do not need to work alone. The presence of actual human partners will make the persona seem more real and believable.
- ***Compliance:*** A digital human influencer/ambassador is just as accountable to legal requirements and platform rules of service as its human counterparts. Always create a persona that plays by the rules.

Some of these goals, especially setting goals, being transparent, and ensuring compliance, are applicable to other digital human personas. But these five will enable a digital influencer/ambassador persona to succeed in an increasingly crowded media world.

The Companion Persona

The third digital human persona, that of a companion, has far different requirements than an assistant. It will need the capacity to answer questions and suggest solutions, but in a much more nuanced and complicated manner. Its core role is to provide *emotional connection and support*, which is a tall order for any system of AI and ML algorithms. But to provide its primary strategic value—*personal engagement and trust*—human users must do two things that are seeming contradictions. First, to consider it a trusted entity, they must personify it to some degree. In the user's mind, it must fulfill the role of a familiar face and voice. Second, and simultaneously, users must not lose sight of the fact that their companion is still a machine, wholly dependent on the data it receives.

COMPANION

Core Role
Emotional Connection and Support

Strategic Value
Personal Engagement and Trust

Key Tech Requirements
Computer Vision, Natural Language Understanding, Sentiment Analysis, Strong Ethical Guardrails

To achieve these paradoxical goals, developers of digital human companions must make careful and thorough use of several AI-based technologies discussed in Chapter 2. These include natural language processing (NLP) and natural language understanding (NLU), used to derive meaning from the user's spoken words as well as the tone or inflection with which the words are said. They must also include computer vision, the AI-enabled means by which a digital human companion can derive meaning from a user's facial expressions and gestures. On top of all this input processing, a viable companion persona should also include the use of affective computing or sentiment analysis, an emerging field that attempts to detect and accurately quantify human feelings.[11]

Clearly, the underlying technology for a truly autonomous companion persona is not yet fully developed. So, for the present, when working one-on-one with a patient or client, digital human companions should always work in close collaboration with their human counterparts. Consider it as a capable coworker, filling in for the qualified professional and extending that professional's reach in situations like routine or remote monitoring. As such, the data used by a companion persona must always remain private, and its output routinely monitored.

Despite the current development state of sophisticated affective computing, there are some current examples of successful companion personas. One of these is XiaoIce,[12] developed by Microsoft and released in 2014. With over 660 million active users and billions of conversations, primarily in China, it is arguably the world's most popular social chatbot. It does not act as an official therapeutic agent for individual patients, but it does employ advanced NLP and sentiment analysis to recognize human emotions and respond accordingly. Xiaolce was built to create an emotional connection with users, satisfying the human need for communication, affection, and social belonging. It was also designed to learn from its experiences, improving its ability to detect and respond to emotional cues.

Another example of the companion persona is Woebot, an AI-enabled chatbot developed at Stanford beginning in 2017. The ongoing project was described in 2020 on Harvard's Digital Innovation and Transformation site:

> **"Woebot[...]is a talk therapy chatbot helping its users monitor their mood and learn about themselves. Using a combination of natural language processing, carefully constructed writing, a sense of humor, and psychological expertise—primarily in Cognitive Behavioral Therapy (CBT), the bot asks its user how they are feeling and how things are going in life in brief daily 10 minute (max) conversations. It then stores all text and emojis and its questions and responses become more specific over time, referencing previous conversations. Like a secret but thoughtful friend and companion in your pocket. The bot addresses mental health and wellness by monitoring its user's mood and need and curating videos and other helpful tools over the chat when relevant."[13]**

Tested extensively during the pandemic, Woebot has proven to be surprisingly effective in helping people deal more effectively with issues such as anxiety, depression, loneliness, and feelings and behaviors related to substance abuse. One study using data from over thirty-six thousand Woebot users found evidence of human-level bonds that were effective in dealing with mental stress.[14] In another study, participants self-reported significant improvements in stress, burnout, and resilience over an eight-week trial, although the researchers recommended further hypothesis-testing studies to draw conclusions about efficacy.[15]

The companion persona represents one of the riskiest examples of deploying digital human agents. For example, if data privacy issues are ignored or the data are exposed, especially in health-related or financial matters, user trust will be irrevocably lost—not to mention the legal liability the developer will incur. This problem becomes more acute as companions move from general, mass audience applications like XiaoIce and Woebot to individual patient or client use cases.

Another hazard to guard against is our tendency to over personalize this type of digital human. In the past, unscrupulous (or perhaps careless) developers have offered digital human companions that created harmful attachments, as described in Chapter 5. Besides developing better AI designed to guard against this, developers need to be completely *transparent* with users, making sure they know they're connecting with an artificial entity, no matter how realistic (and genuinely helpful) that connection may be.

The Digital Twin Persona

This is a type of digital human agent that is easy to imagine (as many science fiction narratives have done) but hard to do in practice. Its core role is to serve as a virtual *replica of a real individual*, acting in that person's place to offer *continuity* and *an authentic offering* of that person's expertise or opinions. This includes many of the attributes of other personas—particularly the emotional connection of a companion—but is identifiable with a real person, not an abstract model of an assistant or a therapist. Sometimes, digital human influencers may also include aspects of the digital twin persona, if they are created as proxies for the real thing.

A relatively well-known example of a digital twin persona is DJK, an AI-based sleep coach.[16] The online persona is based literally on the appearance and expertise of former New Zealand rugby player and current mental health advocate, John Kirwan. Using NLP and 3D modeling technology, DJK offers personalized advice using targeted questions about sleep habits and the user's environment and challenges.

DIGITAL TWIN

Core Role
Virtual Replica of an Individual Person

Strategic Value
Continuity and Authentic Representation

Key Tech Requirements
Expert Knowledge of the Individual, Computer Vision, 3D Rendering, NLP

DJK combines its digital human persona with that of a companion, mimicking the characteristics of the real John Kirwan to enhance the user's comfort and engagement levels. The developer plans to expand DJK's capabilities to address broader mental well-being topics, providing more on demand, nonjudgmental support that can supplement traditional mental health resources.

Other examples of the digital twin persona include the idea of "expert clones," replicas of known authorities like Deepak Chopra[17] and Albert Einstein.[18] Similar in many ways to the digital assistant persons, these are programmed to answer questions in a lifelike, conversational manner, based on the original human's area of expertise. For example, Digital Deepak answers questions (and gives personalized advice) on topics of spirituality, wellness, meditation, and personal growth. Digital Einstein, created to commemorate the one hundredth anniversary of Einstein's Nobel Prize, uses NLP, 3D rendering, and voice synthesis to engage in dialog with users and answer questions about his theories and experiences.

Digital twins have clear roles in supporting healthcare and education, especially when the original human is well-known and/

or has a substantial body of work from which to derive meaningful conversations. However, in order for this persona to serve as a proxy for less well-known experts and professionals, the underlying AI technology will need to become more affordable and versatile.

The Advisor/Coach Persona

This type includes some characteristics of the assistant persona, and even elements of a companion, but is highly focused on helping single, known individuals over extended periods of time. Its core role is to serve as a trusted source for *expertise* and *behavioral guidance*—as they pertain to individual performance. Their value is in facilitating *positive personalized outcomes*. These cover many areas, including one's physical health, finances, job onboarding and performance, or educational progress.

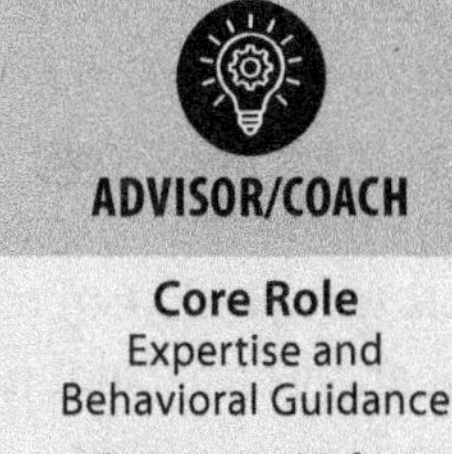

ADVISOR/COACH

Core Role
Expertise and Behavioral Guidance

Strategic Value
Positive Personalized Outcomes

Key Tech Requirements
3D Rendering, Computer Vision, Expert Knowledge, NLP, Sentiment Analysis

In one of these areas—healthcare—there are already AI-enabled digital human platforms serving as supplemental advisors or coaches. Using the AI technologies described in Chapter 2, Atlantis Health's fully customizable digital coach, Ria, provides continuity of support, greater patient engagement, and an empathetic, professional connection.[19] One study found that chatbots and similar digital coaches, while not as genuinely empathetic as a human coach, were more persistent, and could more consistently give patients choices and options to foster their autonomy.[20]

AI-enabled digital humans also fit the advisor/coach persona when it comes to education. For example, Khanmigo from Khan Academy provides personalized tutoring and homework help.[21]

Other systems offer individualized feedback, practice exercises, and explanations outside normal school hours—acting in essence as on-demand study buddies.

In many ways, the advisor persona closely resembles that of a digital assistant—using AI, natural language processing, and related technologies to provide personalized, empathetic recommendations and encouragement. However, the "coach" aspect of this persona may require more sophistication, especially when it involves more creative, higher-cognition performance coaching. To ask open questions, help the client explore his or her potential, and be more than just an information repository, digital humans at this level will need to have advanced deep learning and sentiment analysis capabilities.

There are many other possible personas for digital human agents, of course. These (and their custom cards) are available on the AI Factor Institute website: http://theaifactor.ai.

The Humanity Factor

Dr. Besa Bauta is CIO of the Jewish Board of Family and Human Services and an Assistant Professor at NYU's Silver School of Social Work. She leads the Board's initiatives to design and implement technologies and analytic products that improve the safety, health, and well-being of children and families.

Recently, Dr. Bauta described both her hopes and concerns about the increased use of digital humans in society. Today, she believes, they primarily fill task-oriented roles, such as that of a digital office assistant. However, she also believes the technology will evolve into something much more significant—potentially addressing the "loneliness gap," by providing social and emotional interaction.

Dr. Bauta anticipates a possible future where humans and machines are increasingly blended, certainly through their devices and perhaps even through technologies like neural implants. These agents will mirror our presence and behaviors, essentially "a synthetic version of us, trained on our histories, our memories, and our likes and our dislikes." However, this underscores the need to understand *what makes us uniquely human* in the face of increasingly intelligent AI systems.

While these entities may help us cope with loss and loneliness, they also raise serious psychological and ethical concerns. One is the potential for personalized digital humans to reinforce our *confirmation bias* and contribute to *social isolation*. "The danger is that we're going to be in our own little echo chambers," she explained. "What type of premise does it create when individuals, [especially] young individuals, interact with these platforms in a way where their desires, their wishes are acknowledged, [but] there is no negative feedback?" Such idealized, non-critical entities may well discourage interaction with actual humans.

As digital humans become increasingly adept at mirroring our humanity, Dr. Bauta stresses the importance of exploring the ethical implications of creating and interacting with them. No matter how responsive AI becomes, we must prioritize ways to understand and preserve human connection.

Strategic Integration of Personas

Since we cannot do everything, everywhere, all at once, most organizations must start with the persona that best suits their immediate business goal, using the following flow chart:

While each digital human persona serves a distinct function, aligned with the organization's overall business objective, they are usually most effective when deployed in a coordinated fashion. For example, a *companion* may be used to build trust with a user before referring them to an *advisor*. Similarly, an *assistant* can perform transactions initiated by an *influencer* persona on social media. Likewise, a *digital twin*'s replica of a human expert's

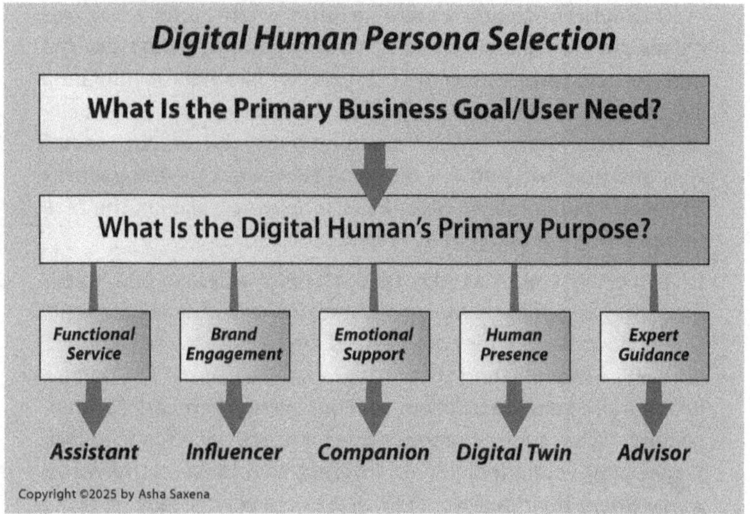

Starting with your organization's primary characteristic (*Optimizer, Extender, Innovator,* or *Multiplier*), identify your digital human's primary purpose to determine its persona.

trusted voice can be embedded within an *advisor* role. This does not mean we must develop an all-in-one, do-everything digital human, but we can develop individual, focused digital human agents with the capacity to work with other agents and their personas. This will ensure that future integrations will allow organizations to provide their members and customers with continuity, relevance, and efficiency.

An example of this future integration—after having first built the appropriate individual apps—would be in the healthcare field. A companion persona could be used for daily emotional check-ins, an advisor or coach persona could be used to inform the patient about CBT techniques, and a digital twin of a known therapist could be used to supplement the actual human, while also coordinating the interactions of the other digital humans. In the retail works, an influencer persona could raise market awareness on social media, referring the interested user to a kiosk-based assistant persona to guide in-store purchases, and to an online advisor persona to recommend personalized regimens. Similarly, in education, a language learning program could integrate a friendly companion or coach persona to walk the learner through each lesson, combined with the user's own digital twin to simulate practice dialogues.

While this may seem like science fiction or fantasy, the integration of these personas have the potential to make digital human agent platforms far exceed the sum of their respective parts. The key ingredient, however, is that digital humans of any persona *must be able to share data between themselves*—while also guarding the user's absolute privacy and humanity. If a companion detects a user's frustration, this insight should inform how the assistant or advisor responds. Likewise, consistency in tone, and a shared memory of all the relevant facts by each digital human persona, will enable organizations to deliver a unified, emotionally intelligent user experience—much like that of a well-coordinated human team.

A Personas-First Strategy

Getting your personas right from the beginning is ***the*** foundation of a viable initiative for incorporating these AI-driven entities into your organization. In the next chapter, we will cover the methodology for creating them, but before doing that, the entire organization must understand who their digital humans are meant to be, and why their personas exist from a purely business perspective.

Deciding on a persona is not a static, onetime-only choice. As the business evolves, and especially as the results of using digital humans become known, the nature of each persona should be reviewed and revisited when building the next version—or a new addition to the group; this is design decision as well as a technical

Ethical Considerations for AI Personas

☑ **Transparency and Explainability**	• Ensure AI decision-making is understandable • Disclose all sources of training data • Clearly inform users they're interacting with AI
☑ **Data Privacy and Protection**	• Obtain explicit user consent • Minimize data collection • Implement secure data storage measures
☑ **Psychological and Emotional Safety**	• Avoid manipulating user emotions • Consider users' mental well-being • Provide feedback channel for all users
☑ **Fairness and Nondiscrimination**	• Regularly audit AI data and results for bias • Ensure inclusive design • Monitor for discriminatory effects
☑ **Compliance with Laws and Regulations**	• Align with all applicable laws and regulations • Maintain audit trails • Verify third-party compliance
☑ **Accountability and Governance**	• Define responsibility for AI actions • Establish ethical oversight

When developing a digital human persona, always consider all the ethical issues.

one. Cross-functional teams including marketing, customer support, IT, and relevant domain experts should always collaborate to define each persona's attributes in detail, including its identity, tone and style, capabilities, and points of integration with other systems. Ideally, a persona definition document will become a guiding blueprint for your developers and their partners.

The benefits of an integrated, personas-first strategy are also *additive*, not isolated or fragmented. By building and then combining the personas of your growing "family" of AI-enabled digital humans, you will be well positioned to cover all four quadrants described in Chapter 6. For example, an ***Optimizer***-based assistant can save costs while an ***Extender***-based influencer can open new markets and drive new revenue. Likewise, an ***Innovator***-based companion can boost loyalty while a wise, ***Multiplier***-based advisor can find new ways to improve user outcomes.

Keep in mind, each persona type comes with the same ethical considerations we discussed in Chapter 5. Each persona must be created with adequate measures taken to avoid undue emotional dependency, guard against bias and data misuse, protect data privacy, and maintain transparency. Doing so will engender trust and loyalty (and make our organizations successful).

A well-defined persona strategy ensures that, when development begins, everyone is clear on our digital humans' purposes—and on the criteria for measuring success.

CHAPTER 8

Developing Digital Humans

In the previous chapter, we described the different personas that define how a digital human agent can act to further our core business objectives. These characteristics can overlap, of course, and a digital human can start out as one type and change over time to become something more. But even though we know these AI-enabled systems are not actual humans, we are drawn to the idea that they are very much like us—after all, the data that creates them comes from us and from the world around us. So, at the risk of over personifying them, let's compare the ***methodology*** for developing and scaling these agents to the process of raising and teaching a child to become a productive member of society. Think of it as ***a progressive journey of learning***, grounded in business strategy and fueled by quality data.

Digital human project teams must include the right balance of business leadership, data expertise, and practical management.

Earlier in this book, and in *The AI Factor*, we explored the foundational principles for developing any artificial intelligence-based system—including digital humans. The roadmap begins with identifying the primary type of business you are in (the Power Quadrant) and its underlying motivations and goals. Next, take every step necessary to ensure that your organization's *data readiness state* is up to the task. This includes everything from executive buy-in and data governance to the composition and aptitude of your entire organization. Digital human project teams, like any other AI project team, must include the right balance of business leadership, data expertise, and practical business management. "Not everyone on the team needs to be a 'data scientist,'...but each role is essential."[1]

Like us, digital humans can follow predictable stages of growth. Even if we don't have children of our own, we recognize this pattern and work towards the best possible end results, in a process we'll call the ***Child-to-Sage (C2S) Model.***™

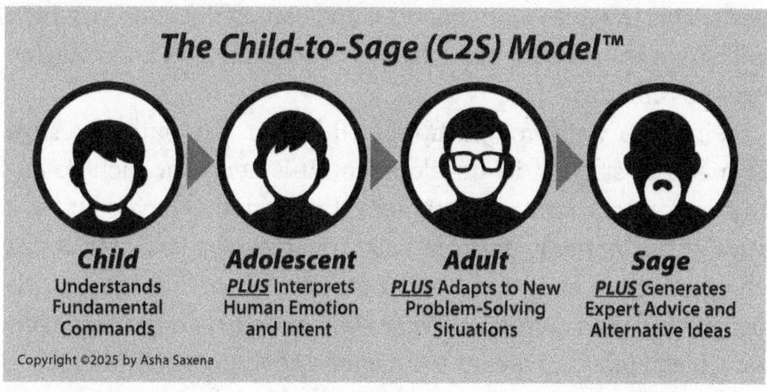

Digital human agents can be characterized in four different stages of development.

The first stage in this process is ***childhood***. Like any human child, digital humans have tremendous potential—an innate foundation—but require close supervision, guidance, and initial training in the basics. While mistakes and unforeseen events are inevitable, the diligence and best practices of the development team will give their digital human agents the best chances to grow into something great.

The first stage is followed by ***adolescence*** and growth. Through repeated experience and feedback, digital human capabilities can expand, and the digital human becomes more competent in performing complex tasks with greater and greater autonomy. However, like human adolescents, it makes mistakes and has much more learning to do. During this stage, members of the development team will also need to grow and expand their own capabilities, in order to meet new challenges and equip their digital human agents to take on new responsibilities.

Then, digital humans can enter the ***adulthood*** stage of development. At this point, they become proficient enough to operate independently, albeit with occasional supervision and feedback. Their actions are based on extensive previous experience and exhaustive knowledge of their field—and of their human counterparts. This involves more nuanced and complex scenarios, which will drive the development team's need to evolve and imagine new possibilities.

Finally, a well-brought up digital human can enter the ***sage*** or maturity stage of its development. It is here that such an entity can provide strategic insights to the team that created it. As a ***sage***, it can not only perform tasks on an expert level, but it can also learn from experience and a vast dataset in order to provide insight and guidance. Like a wise elder or an experienced consultant, it can offer the means to imagine and innovate. At this stage, its developers and users know it is still not perfect, but they need to take advantage of its enormous potential and look for ways to make it even better.

Just as humans require the right food and exercise, digital humans require the right data and a defined business goal.

These stages are not strictly age based. They are also not inevitable. Like any of us, a digital human can remain in the immature ***child*** stage, requiring constant oversight well into their later years. They may even *digress*, becoming less competent and producing more errors. A recent report in *Nature* found that AI systems like ChatGPT and other large language models can collapse, producing more and more errors, when trained on recursively generated data.[2]

For AI systems in general, and especially for digital human agents, the solution is to provide the right training and guidance at every stage of development. Just as a human child, adolescent, adult, and elder requires the right nutrition and exercise in order to thrive, *digital humans need the right data, and the opportunity to act on it to achieve a defined business goal.* In order to progress, it's not simply a matter of supplying digital humans with bigger and bigger datasets and hoping for the best. Rather, in addition to becoming more adept themselves, developers of digital human agents must employ a continuing cycle of iterative learning. They need to stay focused on the business objectives—even when they evolve—and continue to provide robust data management. With a "diet" of high-quality data and a clear purpose, digital humans will continue to grow.

The Digital Human Learning Loop

In 1885, Hermann Ebbinghaus published his findings on the subject of human memory—or rather the lack of it. This was the basis for what we now know as the "forgetting curve," our tendency to rapidly lose new information is there is no attempt to retain it.[3] Technically, AI-based systems cannot really forget things the way we do, but they can fail to learn new and meaningful responses to the data. They "forget" the context of incoming data and thus fail to grow from the ***child*** or ***adolescent*** stage into a more capable entity.

Digital human developers can learn a lot from the ways we humans can overcome the Ebbinghaus "forgetting curve." One of the most frequently mentioned ways for humans to do this is by *spaced repetition*,[4] revisiting the original information and applying it at regular intervals. Similarly, AI-enabled systems can be steadily improved by the repeated use of ***training and feedback loops***. After its initial deployment, a digital human continuously collects data from its interactions, results, and direct user feedback. Ideally, this data is used to refine its model and increase its store of knowledge—always in the context of its overall business objective. When this process is repeated, much like a student reviewing corrections and notes from a teacher or mentor, the digital human can improve its decision-making accuracy. At a point where better responses become the norm, the AI can pass through to the next level of maturity.

This is not a purely linear process, even though it is portrayed that way for clarity's sake. In real-world situations, development stages may overlap, or a system may move back and forth. A digital human may exhibit ***adult*** capabilities in some areas while still being an ***adolescent*** in others, depending on the quality of the data and the complexity of the assigned tasks. This framework is flexible, encouraging teams to evaluate a digital human's performance *continuously*. It should only progress to the next stage and assume broader responsibilities when it consistently excels at its current duties.

In practical terms, this means establishing performance metrics at each stage and using them to decide if the digital human

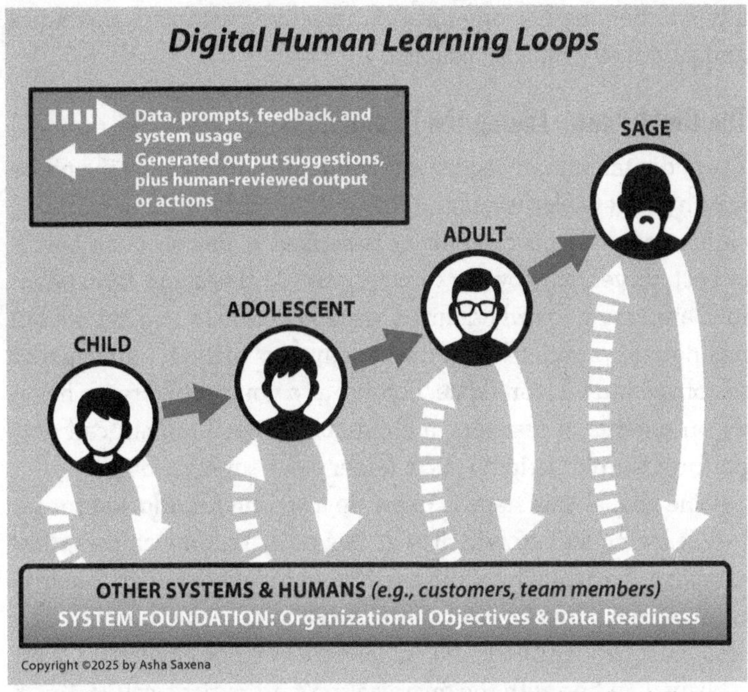

As a digital human agent receives and incorporates valid feedback data from interactions with its human counterparts, it can advance to a higher level of autonomy.

is ready to take on more. These must include response accuracy, user satisfaction scores, and error rates, among others. As we go through each of the four stages, we will highlight the kinds of data and feedback involved, and how it can reinforce learning.

We will also illustrate each phase with a hypothetical example of an AI-enabled entity being used in a business context. For our purposes, we will follow a digital human customer service agent, Ada, and her progress from infancy to maturity at a fictitious Acme Corporation. As her knowledge and skills grow, such a digital human can progress from answering basic FAQs to becoming an expert virtual assistant to eventually becoming a strategic advisor, helping her organization improve customer experience and gain new business insights.

The Child Phase: Laying the Foundations

Every digital human begins as a ***child***, the earliest learning phase for any AI-enabled system. (Without AI and machine learning, earlier data systems can only be described as preconscious beings at best, driven only by our direct input.) At this stage, its capabilities are very narrowly defined, usually confined to a simple but business-appropriate objective. It employs artificial intelligence to collect and interpret data, but just as a young child relies heavily on parents or teachers, a child-stage digital human can only perform simple, scripted tasks under close supervision.

The goal at this stage is to create a ***strong foundation*** for future learning and growth. It is at this point that developers must establish the digital human's basic persona, even though that may change over time. Of course, the sources of viable training data also must be identified, and initial performance expectations established, in line with the organization's primary objective.

Typically, a digital human in the ***child*** stage typically interacts with users in a highly constrained manner. Its conversational ability is straightforward and literal, making it clear to the user that they are working with an AI. It can answer a predefined set of frequently asked questions and execute basic instructions, but they cannot handle unexpected input. This is much like a toddler who can recite the alphabet but cannot have a complex conversation.

At this point, the digital human is often strictly rules based. It is supported by a modest machine learning model and trained on a small, curated dataset. Its intelligence is ***narrowly focused*** and entirely learned from what the AI has been explicitly given during training.

Because of these limitations, human oversight is critical. The digital human ***child's*** outputs must be reviewed frequently by those familiar with its business objective and its impact on the organization. Early on, it might be allowed to operate only in a sandbox environment or in a limited deployment situation. (For example, in the early stages, a digital human might be made available to a small user group or be charged with handling only internal queries to ensure that any mistakes have minimal impact.) In effect, the organization should treat the AI initially as a trainee or intern.

At this stage, learning is primarily a ***one-way process***. Developers and early users teach the digital human using training data, scripted dialogues, or decision trees. Feedback from real interactions is initially minimal, since the system usually is not widely available to users at first. However, even in pilot tests, capturing user reactions and errors is critical, since it will lead to further improvements.

Once the initial deployment has proven successful, a digital human at the ***child*** stage can be used more broadly and used by the entire population of customers or other constituents. But like an actual child, ***its activities must still be limited to well-defined activities***, like answering basic questions and escalating complex ones to human teammates. Even so, the data collected from these limited activities is incredibly valuable. It can become the basis for other digital humans, including the current ***child*** to advance to the next stage.

The Role and Nature of the Data

In the ***child*** stage, data should be seen as ***basic curriculum*** for its learning and development. The agent's AI is usually trained on historical question and answer pairs, product information, knowledgebase articles, and similar preexisting data. This means it is vital to ensure that the data is of the highest quality, unbiased, and free from privacy concerns. As with any other artificial intelligence system, errors or bias in the training data will affect the behavior of the digital human agent. This is where the *data readiness status* of your organization will pay off. By ensuring that you use ***clean, relevant, and well-structured data***, you will efficiently train a digital human's first version and prepare it to move to the next phase.

Ada's First Steps

Acme Corporation has a far-reaching sales and marketing operation, including an e-commerce platform, a network of independent retailers, and global distribution for thousands of products. Needless to say, customer service is a major cost center. As an initial pilot project, the company deployed their digital human, Ada, as a simple chatbot on the company's website. She would answer questions such as "What is your return policy?" or "How do I track my order?" Her AI was trained on the company's help center articles and FAQs. When a customer asks for information that is outside her knowledge, Ada would respond with a polite, programmed answer, "I'm sorry. I can't handle that request at this time."

This is normal behavior at the ***child*** stage; Ada is still ***learning boundaries***. The development team monitors these interactions, looking for questions she cannot answer, such as "Can I return an item after thirty days?" They note the gap and either add the appropriate answer to Ada's store of information or adjust her algorithms. This is a simple, early example of a ***feedback loop*** in action. At this stage, every failure or user frustration is treated as a learning opportunity to fine-tune Ada's responses. It is also typical of the ***supervised learning*** process. Just as a teacher would correct a child's mistake, the developers correct Ada by updating her training data or rules.

The ***child*** stage may last a while, through an extended pilot period, for example, until Ada can reliably handle the assigned scope of work. However, once she achieves the project targets, such as handling most FAQ questions consistently, with high user satisfaction levels for those interactions, it's a sign that Ada is ready to "grow up" into the next phase.

It's worth noting that many AI projects just *stop* at this ***child***-like level—a basic chatbot that never really improves. Such stagnation is contrary to the Digital Human Learning Loop framework. Just as leaving a child untaught would squander their potential, ***leaving a digital human at the child stage means that you are not realizing the full value of AI***. To unlock greater potential value, we must guide digital humans through adolescence and beyond by leveraging data from real interactions.

Adolescence: Learning and Expansion

At the ***adolescent*** stage, digital humans begin to realize their potential. Having mastered the basics, the underlying AI now begins to learn from experience, expand its knowledge, and handle more complexity. Like a teenager gaining competency and independence, there is growth and excitement, but also occasional missteps that require guidance. For a digital human, this stage is a period of rapid improvement driven by continuous training data, user feedback, and iterative refinement of algorithms.

In the ***adolescent*** phase, digital human capabilities broaden significantly. It can manage a much wider range of queries or tasks than it could in the ***child*** stage, including some dynamic or multi-turn interactions. The AI's language understanding and responses become more natural and context aware; it may start to recognize user intent, even if questions are phrased in novel ways.

Up until now, it is very likely that a digital human would use a chatbot-like text or voice interface. But at the ***adolescent*** stage, developers may want to consider the digital human's visual appearance—even if it won't be fully implemented until the ***adult*** stage. Adding a humanlike avatar should not be done because it is novel or trendy; rather, it gives the agent a far better way to know someone's level of satisfaction (or frustration), by interpreting their tone of voice and facial expression, and responding appropriately. Using natural language programming and computer vision, the digital human can acquire an enormous amount of AI training data.

Like any adolescent, a digital human at this level is not yet an expert. Errors and knowledge gaps still occur in unfamiliar situations. The digital human might occasionally provide an incorrect answer or escalate to a human agent for very complex issues. The key difference from the prior stage is that now the AI can learn from these mistakes with less human intervention required in the learning loop. The benefits of a self-improving system are clear. The more users engage with the digital human, the smarter it gets over time, provided that the data are captured and fed back to the AI.

Data and Feedback Loops

The ***adolescent*** stage is heavily driven by feedback loops. At this point, the digital human is interacting with real users on a regular basis, generating a wealth of conversational data. Every user query and corresponding AI answer can be logged and analyzed. Developers (or automated training pipelines) use this data to fine-tune the AI's models. For example, if a digital human frequently misunderstands a particular type of request, the pattern can be identified. The AI can then be retrained with better examples for that case. This stage involves techniques like ***reinforcement learning*** or active learning, where the AI is gradually trained to maximize a reward, such as success in answering without fallback, or a high customer rating.

To measure results and feed data back into the AI, it is important to have a ***user feedback mechanism***. For example, after an interaction is complete, simply ask, "Did I answer your question?" and capture the answer. Those signals become labels that help

the AI distinguish good versus bad performance. Over hunc or thousands of such interactions, the digital human's skill l can improve, much like a teenager learning from each new s or classroom experience.

Another vital aspect of this phase is that the digital humar start integrating with ***new data sources***. Instead of being li to static data, like articles and FAQ lists, the system can be nected to live constantly changing databases or systems. range from order management and product databases to cus histories and preferences—gathered with permission, of c With more data to learn from, the digital human can detec nuanced patterns and provide more sophisticated response

An organization's ***data readiness*** plays a crucial role process. Any new dataset or system integrated with the human's AI must be well governed, accessible, secure, an authorized. Doing so will not only enhance the AI's perfor it will also engender trust and lead to better, more reliable versions of digital humans. Teaching an ***adolescent*** digital to follow the rules of good data governance will lead to be sults in adulthood.

Teen Ada's Debut

After a successful pilot program, Acme rolls out Ada to all tomers, not only on the website but also on its mobile sl app. Now, she not only answered FAQs, but can also h tomers check on their order status, process return reque recommend products from the catalog. For example, sh answer a question that fell outside a predetermined script a gift for my mother's birthday, she likes gardening. Any tions?" In the ***child*** stage, Ada couldn't handle such requ now, as an ***adolescent*** AI, Ada could respond, "Sure! For ing enthusiasts, our top-rated gift is the Smart Irrigation send you more details or other gardening gift ideas."

This more fluid, contextual response reveals Ada's growing ompetence, achieved through ***iterative improvements***. Customrs routinely made requests for product suggestions—a pattern hat was easily detected, but Ada's initial product suggestions ere hit-or-miss. The team then trained Ada, not just on the roduct data but on the customers' responses to her suggestions. s a result, Ada learned how to recommend products that cusomers were more likely to buy.

During this stage, Ada also developed a bit of a "personality"—ne consistent with her persona design. For instance, if a user as upset about a delayed shipment, Ada learned to recognize the entiment and offer an apology with empathy. In one interaction, customer angrily says, "This is the second time my order has een late! What is going on?" Initially, Ada responded with geeric tracking info, which didn't help, and the customer provided low rating. The team used that feedback to teach Ada to first acnowledge the frustration, saying something like, "I'm really sorry bout the delay. Let me check what happened with your order." ow Ada's responses feel more human and caring, building a beter rapport.

This training in handling emotional cues reflects recent reearch that found, even if we know a digital human isn't real, we ill react to it as if it were. We are attuned to and react emotionly to facial signals and cues.[5] By incorporating those humanlike ements into Ada's behavior, Acme Corp made the experience ore engaging for users.

By the end of the *adolescent* stage, Ada has become a capable rtual assistant for the company. She can handle the majority customer inquiries across multiple contexts, including inforational questions, transactional requests, basic troubleshooting, nd simple recommendations. The need to hand off requests to a uman has dropped substantially, from about 50 percent of the

exchanges in the ***child*** stage to around 20–30 percent, typically for only the most complex issues.

This has tangible benefits for Acme: Customers can get instant help at any time, and the human support team is free to focus on truly difficult cases. Firms that embrace digital humans at this level can substantially lower costs, increase revenues and gain a sustainable first mover advantage over their competitors. Customers may even become attached to their digital helpers over time and thus become more loyal to the brand.

Once Ada has become more reliable in her area of responsibility, handling 85–90 percent of support queries with high customer satisfaction, for example, then she is ready for even greater responsibilities. When a digital human agent exceeds average human performance in such tasks, it is a sign that it's time to move to the ***adult*** stage.

Adulthood: Expertise and Autonomy

A digital human ***adult*** is one that has reached a high level of proficiency and autonomy, comparable to that of a skilled human professional. At this point, the underlying AI has accumulated vast amounts of information—through the previous stages' learning loops as well as its connections to many other data sources. As a result, it is capable of handling more nuanced, complex tasks. It can also act more independently, with minimal human intervention. Its decisions can be trusted, for the most part, within the agent's specific domain expertise.

At this stage, a digital human's conversational abilities are more refined; dialogues feel natural, coherent, and contextually aware over long interactions. The AI can manage multi-turn conversations that require memory of earlier parts of the dialogue. It understands complex language constructs, can disambiguate user intents, and can provide detailed, correct information—even when questions are open-ended. In some cases, it may even begin to be proactive, anticipating what a user might need next and suggest it without being asked.

If such a digital human has performed well in its ***childhood*** and ***adolescence***, it is far more likely to be trusted with critical operations. There must still be human oversight, via monitoring of AI metrics and occasional performance audits, but such digital humans are able to operate on their own.

The Role of Data and Continuous Learning

It's easy to think that for a digital human who has reached the ***adult*** stage, the need for intensive learning would be far less. On the contrary, ***learning becomes more continuous and fine-grained***. The difference is that the AI learning process is largely ***unsupervised***. The development team can introduce automated retraining pipelines that periodically update the AI model with fresh data, incrementally improving its performance accuracy and updating its enormous store of information. This process can also be designed to self-correct or at least issue an alert when it encounters an unknown condition.

Although routine matters within the digital human's area of expertise have become more automatic, its autonomy still has limits. Whenever the AI's decisions carry more potential risk, such as actions affecting a customer's finances or healthcare, there must be an increased emphasis on ***data governance and ethics***. Human teams must ensure that data drifts or biases have not crept in—not to mention interference from bad actors.

At the ***adult*** stage, a digital human can perform tasks more efficiently than humans, even when unsupervised. But it still does not possess human judgment or discernment. Its actions are governed solely by the quality and the integrity of the data it receives. At this stage, there is an even greater need for fairness and good governance in practice, which means there must be regular audits of the digital human's output.

In essence, the ***adult*** stage of a digital human involves ***maintaining excellence***. This means that the flow of data must be used to fine-tune AI performance, but it also means that the AI must be prevented from causing harm.

Ada, the Trusted Associate

By now, Ada has been operating for some time and has interacted with millions of customers. Through continuous improvement, she has become exceptionally skilled at customer service and as a sales associate, available not just in chat and the mobile app, but also on voice calls and as an avatar in store kiosks.

A Typical Interaction

Ada is capable of handling multiple, simultaneous interactions with customers at a consistently high level. For example, a customer we'll call Grace might initiate a conversation with a complex question. "Hi Ada. I bought a smart sprinkler system from you guys last month, and it's acting up. It was supposed to adjust based on weather, but it isn't. Can you help?" The request involves a specific product, a technical issue, and possibly warranty service. Drawing on her extensive knowledgebase, Ada identifies the customer, and everything related to the purchased product. She replies, "Hi Grace! I'm sorry your SmartSprinkle 3000 isn't working as expected. Let's get that fixed. I see you bought it in July, so it's under warranty. First, can you tell me if it's connected to your Wi-Fi and if the weather data feature is enabled in the app?" Ada not only pulled up Grace's purchase record (an integration with the CRM and order system), but also applied troubleshooting steps (from the product support database), all in a friendly, conversational tone. She even showed initiative, preemptively checking the warranty status.

Grace responds with the details, and Ada guides her through a few diagnostic steps. When it becomes clear that the device might be defective, Ada immediately initiates a replacement order. "It looks like this might be a hardware issue. I've initiated a free replacement order to your address on file. You'll get a confirmation email shortly, and it should arrive within five business days. I've also scheduled a reminder to check in after it arrives, to make sure it's working. Is there anything else I can help you with?"

This resolution is something a top-notch human agent would deliver, but Ada handled it end to end instantly. Grace rates the interaction five stars, and even says "Thank you," to which Ada responds, "You're welcome! Happy to help, and I hope the new unit works perfectly. Have a great day!"

In this example, Ada is operating as an autonomous agent, accessing databases, making decisions, and providing empathetic service. Her behavior also generates new data for Acme—identifying a potentially defective product. Aggregating such cases, Ada can later report common failure patterns to the engineering team, or alert them if a particular batch of devices has issues. Digital humans at this level can be a rich source of knowledge, contributing insights and identifying trends from thousands of interactions that individual humans might miss.

The key benefits at this stage are scale and consistency. Ada has essentially graduated to being a core part of the team—providing insights and possible solutions as well as handling tasks with minimal oversight. For many organizations, digital humans at the ***adult*** stage are "good enough" for their intended purpose. Ethical and operational oversight is still a factor, but the decision to progress to the next stage will depend on whether giving the AI a more high-level, strategic role truly supports the organization's core objectives.

The Sage: Wisdom and Strategic Guidance

A digital human agent at the maturity or ***sage*** level represents the pinnacle of AI development, and perhaps even evidence of artificial general intelligence (or AGI). As the closest possible simulation of human wisdom, within its domain, a ***sage***-level digital human can leverage that capability to advise, innovate, and even lead its human counterparts. If the ***adult*** level is about *doing things right*, the ***sage*** level is about *doing the right things*.

At the ***sage*** level, the digital human possesses at least an expert-level understanding of its domain, including its context, history, and nuances that even human experts might take years to master. It is capable of synthesizing information from many sources and providing insight. A ***sage***-level AI can handle highly ambiguous queries, solve novel problems by drawing analogies to past knowledge, and generate creative solution possibilities. The ***sage*** stage also implies a degree of proactivity and foresight. It does not need to wait to be asked; it can proactively supply important information or warnings. It can also learn continuously, in real time, from new data streams.

Another characteristic is its role in an organization. At this stage, such a digital human might even be given a seat at the table in decision-making forums. At strategy meetings, it could provide data-driven recommendations, or it might mentor employees by sharing best practices learned from data. This requires that its human counterparts evolve as well, not just in their capacity to work with such high-speed, continuously learning partners but also in their role as arbiters of human values. No matter how powerful a ***sage***-level digital human may become, it is still a product of its data. As such, it must always have truly ethical human partners.

Data Rules!

To reach ***sage*** status, an AI needs extensive and diverse data. Typically, the feedback loop extends beyond its immediate interactions. To create a full understanding, it must also draw on external and historical data, as well as any information related, however remotely, to the subject domain. Data reinforcement at this stage might involve analyzing long-term trends, incorporating research or expert knowledge into the AI's model, and even simulating multiple scenarios.

At this stage, the AI might use predictive analytics to foresee future outcomes. For example, it might predict a customer's future needs or forecast market trends from patterns in the data. The feedback loop here can become very sophisticated: the AI's own insights can be validated against real outcomes and the results fed back to refine the AI's strategic models. Essentially, the AI is learning not just from direct feedback ("was this answer right or wrong?") but from consequences over time ("did our decision lead to success or failure over the quarter/year?").

Achieving this will require that an organization has a very mature data culture—that data from all parts of the organization is accessible and used to train the AI. It also means that the data must include every other aspect of sound governance, including policies for its safe and beneficial use.

Wise Ada

Let's continue with our Ada example to imagine her as a ***sage***. Having mastered customer service and sales, her wealth of interaction data and experience is now being leveraged for higher-level tasks. Acme leadership had decided to upgrade her role to that of an internal advisor for customer service business strategy. Ada has conversed with millions of customers and knows intimately their pain points and desires. At this stage, Ada might produce a report concluding, "In the past month, 30 percent of our customers asking about product X have ended up asking for a refund due to difficulty using it. I recommend a redesign of the setup process for product X." Such insight is proactive and strategic: Ada is essentially pointing out an opportunity for product line improvement, something done traditionally by human analysts or product managers. But because Ada can analyze all customer dialogues at scale, she catches these trends early and often.

Reaching the ***sage*** stage often involves leveraging the latest AI advancements. For Ada, Acme might incorporate a powerful language model, fine-tuned on all of Acme's data, not on public data subject to errors and bias. This would effectively give Ada the ability to reason, project likely outcomes, and generate sophisticated answers.

The risk at this stage is ensuring the AI remains aligned with company values and goals. A digital human that is completely autonomous might propose strategies that conflict with human intuition or ethical standards. Therefore, even an agent at the ***sage*** level should have ***governance guardrails***. In practice, this means that, while Ada can make recommendations, humans will still review major decisions. But with that in mind, ***sage*** level can be characterized as ***a partnership between human experts and AI***—combining human creativity and judgment with AI's analytical superpowers.

The Role of Data and Feedback Loops

Across all stages of digital human development, there is one constant: the importance of data as fuel for advancement. The Digital Human Learning Loop relies, fundamentally, on feedback loops, where output data is fed back as input for improvement. This not only reinforces learning, it also facilitates the transitions between stages:

From Child to Adolescent – Early stage digital humans learn from static training data. But the transition to the ***adolescent*** stage occurs when the AI begins to learn from dynamic interaction data. User queries, whether or not the AI answers were helpful or relevant, become new training examples. At this point, there must be a feedback collection mechanism, capturing answers, unanswered questions, and qualitative ratings. By analyzing this feedback, developers can improve algorithms and expand the AI's knowledge. This is largely a human in the loop process. The better an organization is at collecting and using this data, the faster a digital human will learn and advance to the next level.

From Adolescent to Adult: During the ***adolescent*** phase, the sheer volume of interactions grows exponentially, making manual review of each one impractical. Here, the feedback loop must include analytics and automation, tracking such metrics as success rates, confusion triggers, or average handling time. Also, with so many individual interactions, many of which consist of unstructured data, more advanced machine learning (such as deep learning NLP models) must be employed. The transition to the ***adult*** stage is facilitated by introducing *learning automation*. However, human experts must still be involved—to make sure the AI does not learn incorrect behavior from one-off mistakes or malicious inputs. There are ***diminishing returns*** inherent in the direct human training of AI models, but there are ***increasing returns*** possible through the use of data-driven, self-learning artificial intelligence systems.

From Adult to Sage: By the time an AI-enabled digital human has reached the ***adult*** stage, it will have to be integrated with many processes, each requiring a high level of data readiness. The feedback loop in this case is more about ***outcome data*** and ***long-term learning***. Ultimately, if these long-term findings are interpreted by a robust, highly sophisticated AI, the digital human that encompasses them will be capable of making wise, contextual predictions and recommendations—a trusted ***sage*** and partner. It closes the loop; the AI does not learn solely from immediate corrections or variations in the data, but from the real-world impact of its actions. User engagement remains vital. Even if the digital human gives sound, strategic advice, humans must always be present. "Does this make sense?" "Is it aligned with our purpose?" "Is it aligned with our values?" This too will help fine-tune the AI's "wisdom," ensuring that it become an even more valued partner.

Across all these transitions, several themes stand out. A successful digital human project always treats data as a ***continuous stream***, not a onetime resource. From day one, plan how data from the AI's interactions will be collected, stored, and fed back for improvement. This means that good ***data quality and governance*** are *indispensable*. In addition, the data used in digital human projects will always guide *when* to progress to the next level. This means ***incremental expansion***, learning how to employ a digital human solution in your area of the Power Quadrant before attempting something more ambitious. Finally, the value of ***human feedback*** and ***hybrid approaches*** to digital human projects cannot be underestimated. Even with great data and procedures, human insight is invaluable at every stage. When used wisely and often, it can make any digital human partnership a lasting, virtuous cycle.

CHAPTER 9

Practical Advice

Just as AI itself has increased in importance with amazing speed, so also have digital human agents—entities that mimic our behavior and promise to change everything about how we live and work. For some, this idea is frightening. For others, it is the beginning of a new area in human productivity. But unlike older technology disruptions (the steam engine or the telephone, for example), the *velocity* of change is increasing at a far greater pace. With seemingly no time to catch our breath, we need to hear from experts we can trust—professionals who have been working with AI and digital agents for years. They also need to be trustworthy, experts who are not trying to sell us something.

In preparing this book, I spoke with many such experts, some of whose views are included in earlier chapters. But their consensus on digital human agents is so powerful that I have included the others in a separate chapter, one that should inspire confidence in the future of digital human partnerships.

Two Intelligences, Working Together

Dan Turchin is the CEO of PeopleReign, developers of a virtual agent platform for HR and IT operations. Their multilingual, multichannel agent is preconfigured to understand millions of common work concepts and, when the agent is unable to resolve the issue autonomously, automatically routes the request to most suitable live agent—with a recommendation of the best next action.

Turchin emphasized that AI-based digital humans and actual humans operate under two different types of intelligence—the former being based in memorization and task-specific execution and the latter highlighting empathy and rational judgement. Notwithstanding, he believes that the two can participate in partnership, emphasizing *augmentation* rather than replacement of human jobs. "Bots are best suited to perform tasks; humans are best suited to do jobs." He also noted that this arrangement is nothing new, stressing the fact that those who embrace technology just evolve faster. "Ever since our use of fire or the internet, we have had tools to help us do our jobs; AI is only the latest tool."

Leading teams that develop such digital agents require a high level of transparency on how and why decisions are made, Turchin maintained. This will ensure user control over the data, and over the predictability and configurability of the AI's work.

There is significant risk posed by bad actors amplifying *their* capabilities through AI, Turchin concludes. However, digital human agents also have the potential to augment *our* abilities, giving us the means to better address major global challenges.

The Power of Procedural Knowledge

Amit Prakash is the cofounder and CEO of A79, an AI startup headquartered in the US, and the cofounder of ThoughtSpot, an agentic analytics platform. In 2024, ThoughtSpot introduced

Spotter, an agentic AI analyst that allows customers to converse with it as they would with a human analyst. Regardless of their technical expertise level, users can ask a question in natural language, get an answer from the company's store of information and procedures, and ask follow-up questions.

Digital agents' decision-making ability will accelerate problem solving [but also] increase the potential for inequity. However, these same tools can be used to solve the problems they create.

Prakash defines agents by their ability ***to independently plan and make high-level decisions*** in order to achieve specified goals. In his words, an agent can "take a high-level goal, come up with plan to achieve that goal, and be able to make a lot of higher-level decisions on its own, as opposed to requiring a human to specify them." This will both accelerate problem-solving and increase the potential for weaponization and inequity. However, he also hopes that these same tools can be used to solve the problems they create.

He asserted that while LLMs have benefited from the vast repository of *descriptive knowledge* on the internet, the key missing piece for advanced AI agents is ***documented procedural knowledge***. This includes the "how-to" knowledge derived from human experience. Its absence creates a serious problem. "With today's LLMs, 60 percent of the time it might be giving you the right answer," he noted, "but the remaining 40 percent of the time it may be giving you a random answer, and that's just not acceptable."

Descriptive or declarative knowledge (the "what") includes facts, concepts, relationships, and principles that represent what is true across a wide range of situations. Procedural knowledge is the "how-to" side of the equation, representing the skills, methods, and processes for accomplishing goals. It is typically more complex than descriptive or conceptual knowledge.[1] It is also often domain specific, and can be poorly documented, making it far more difficult to incorporate into agentic systems. But without it, digital human agents are merely information banks, without the ability to direct users or formulate relevant, high-level decisions.

Overall productivity gains from AI agents are modest today, he accepts, due to limited computing power and the absence of procedural data. However, there will be exponential productivity increases in the coming years. For enterprises, he advises companies to bet on the people they partner and cocreate with, rather than waiting for a packaged solution.

A Question of Balance

Jeffrey Garwood is the senior VP of Strategy at the AI Factor Institute and former vice president of Architecture and Solutions at Salesforce. There, he led teams of software architects and data specialists in developing AI and CRM technologies for financial services and healthcare organizations.

On the topic of digital humans (and AI in general), Garwood advocates for a more balanced development approach, one that prioritizes both efficiency and adaptability. Teams creating these agents must have not only technical and data expertise. They must also have a strong understanding of human behavior and cognitive processes. "You need people that understand people, because you're trying to capture humanlike behavior."

From past experience, Garwood knows that digital human agents are already well suited to take on repetitive and tedious tasks. They can process and analyze data more broadly than humans can, providing deeper insights. Digital humans "could help us do certain things better than we could have otherwise done ourselves," he noted. "It might do some things independently… better than we can do ourselves." But he is also well aware of the negative potential.

Digital humans have the potential to fundamentally change the way we work, think, behave, and organize.

One of these is that our overreliance on digital humans may lead to a decline in critical reasoning and thinking skills. "It may make people too lax in trusting what's given them," he said. Another potential risk is a failure to define the boundaries of digital humans' actions, ensuring that they operate ethically and within predefined limits. He asked, "How do you balance what [the digital human] is doing, and then what it's doing *independently*? How do we monitor, engage, and control that?"

In Garwood's view, digital humans have the potential to fundamentally change the way we work, think, behave, and organize. "What's going to be fundamentally different," he remarked, "is that [digital humans] are going to start doing things we didn't picture them doing or adding things we didn't think were possible."

First Things First

David Bader is a Distinguished Professor and the Director of the Institute for Data Science at the New Jersey Institute of Technology. He is also cofounder of Adapter, a startup adapting the world to you. Adapter is "mission control" for your life experiences, helping you streamline decisions, reduce noise, and amplify what matters. Adapter is ultra-personalized and tailors your world, finding and booking activities—from flights to dinner—that perfectly match your unique preferences and lifestyle.

In a recent interview, Bader stressed the need to develop digital agents that can meet specific, known objectives before moving on to more ambitious projects. He also recommended that development teams focus on cost models and total cost of ownership—not just capabilities. "It's very easy to admire the capabilities that you can put inside this product" he explained.

"What is not well understood or thought through yet, is the cost for doing so."

Digital humans also will operate under a very different economic model than human employees, which will involve licensing and potentially different pricing structures for products and services.

The essential steps in creating digital humans are to first identify the tasks that can be automated in a cost-effective manner, then to address the technical challenges related to knowledge, context, and company values. "First, find the tasks where we think it more cost effective to have a digital human than a real person," he noted, "but also [operate] within the values of the company."

Bader stressed the urgency for companies to proactively engage with digital human technology to avoid being left behind. "Companies have to be engaged with digital humans, with AI agents," he added. "[They must] understand how they are going to employ them, use them, and redesign their company around this new digital world."

Augmenting Ourselves

Ankur Khanna is vice president for Data, Analytics, and Technology at L'Oréal, where he leads teams involved in the company's IT strategy and AI integration. In a recent interview, he emphasized the practical value of digital agents in augmenting what we do. "I don't want to compare them to humans, to be honest," he noted, viewing digital humans as augmented humans with significantly enhanced productivity, "almost like a ten times boost in what they're able to accomplish."

Khanna sees the primary benefit in freeing up humans to focus on "more complex, more value-added tasks," particularly critical thinking and problem-solving. He also observed the capacity of AI-powered representatives to create new business models and "make money while you're sleeping," borrowing Warren Buffett's famous saying on investment strategy.

"For the most part, it should help us get better at our jobs and weed out the ones who don't get comfortable with this tech."

Within the next three to five years, Khanna foresees that digital humans will primarily *augment* jobs rather than replace them. Beyond that, there will be workforce shifts and displacements, compelling more people to adapt. "For the most part, it should help us get better at our jobs and weed out the ones who don't get comfortable with this tech." There is also the potential for humans to lose creative abilities and critical thinking skills due to overreliance on the technology, but he maintains that digital human agents will be a net positive in the long-term.

The *composition* of teams that develop and use digital human agents is of utmost importance. Khanna opined that such teams need the "usual suspects"—software engineers and data scientists. But they also need "translators," those who understand both the technical aspects of AI as well as the business domain issues, and who can effectively bridge that gap. He also stressed the need to "storyboard" projects, making their goals and methods clear to all stakeholders. For consumer applications, smart, affordable, and privacy-respecting AI is essential. For work applications, the team must develop digital personas tailored to specific business roles and with clear accountability structures.

Define the Use Case!

Meena Mallipeddi is the CEO of AmplifyMD, developer of an AI-enhanced automation and communication platform for healthcare providers. In addition to its HIPAA-compliant communication and order-entry capabilities, AmplifyMD is actively developing AI-powered solutions for delivering better and faster care while also reducing administrative burdens.

In a recent interview, Mallipeddi described how many hospitals are moving toward a "virtual sitting service," to help monitor patients and reduce nurse workload, using AI for patient alerts. While initial feedback has been positive, the various agents on the market today currently require human oversight, due to limitations in technology and standards—such as precise fall risk detection. However, the ultimate goal is full automation of the monitoring process, allowing a single nurse to oversee more patients. The concept of remote monitoring and hybrid work involving agents and humans is not limited to healthcare, she noted. "It will revolutionize how care is delivered in the hospital completely, because you will get more personalized care. But it's also going to be a hybrid of in person and virtual in other areas. I think we're going to see a lot more of that across all of our lives...."

As digital agents become more pervasive, we will need new management paradigms, to realize new opportunities and to guard against overreliance on our digital counterparts.

Mallipeddi emphasized the need for development teams of experienced professionals who understand the pros and cons of AI, the risks of improper training (such as hallucinations and bias), and the importance of building in safeguards to prevent misuse by bad actors. But an absolutely essential aspect of digital human development is to clearly ***define the use case***, especially for high-stakes applications like medical diagnosis. "Be very clear on the use case, on the inputs you need, and on all the ways that it can go wrong," she stressed. "Make sure that all aspects are clearly written down beforehand, and what you're expecting [to find]."

As digital human agents become more pervasive, Mallipeddi believes that we will need new management paradigms, involving hybrid teams of humans and digital agents equipped to realize new opportunities and guard against overreliance on our digital counterparts. "AI is going to be this amazing, revolutionary thing that we can't even imagine today," she said. "Looking out twenty years [from now], we just don't know what life is going to be like, because we don't even know all the use cases involved."

An Authentic Digital Identity

Eman Kawas is the cofounder of Thynkli, a data analytics and "Digital Twin as a Service" developer. Based in Vancouver and Dubai, her company works with energy and infrastructure companies (among others) to improve operations and skill levels through automation and artificial intelligence.

Kawas draws an important distinction between true digital humans—particularly, digital twins—and ordinary chatbots, and other existing AI tools. The latter, she maintains, have a very specific and limited scope, allowing them to replicate *some* tasks within a process, like screening job candidates or conducting initial interviews. This makes today's chatbots only *vaguely* comparable to actual humans. What they lack is a *distinct digital identity* which would not only distinguish it from basic chatbots, but it would also enable them to accomplish their full potential. When used in the context of a digital twin, it would:

- ***Mitigate trust issues and verify thoughts:*** A digital identity would act as a "passport" of sorts that can verify the origin of its output. This is crucial for building trust and addressing concerns about whether a response is genuinely human in nature or generated by AI.
- ***Provide grounding and prevent bias:*** An authentic digital identity serves as a "core" that would allow the digital human to process information with a foundation of a human's character, beliefs, and diverse experiences. This would help prevent the creation of bias.

- ***Ensure consistency*** – The identity, derived from understanding a human's unique character, cultural beliefs, and thought processes, would act like a "stem cell," ensuring consistency in the digital human's interactions and outputs, regardless of how much further data or analysis is built upon it.
- ***Enable the replication of human thinking:*** A digital identity is foundational to the broader vision of creating a digital replica, "capable of thinking and producing output" across different subjects and contexts. It allows for augmenting human capabilities and thinking processes on a larger scale.

Kawas acknowledged that such a system of authentic digital identities would present its own challenges when it comes to trust. Such challenges, she noted, "can be mitigated if we leverage the right technology; blockchain is one of them."

Creating a digital twin with an authentic digital identity is a multifaceted problem, combining a clear definition of the digital human's role with advanced verification and dynamic security protection. For example, a digital human as a healthcare agent might need HIPAA-compliant identity credentials. Doing so consistently could require that developers assign biometric- and/or blockchain-based identifiers, to prove the agent's origin, ownership, and authorization scope.[2]

Guarding Against Cyberattacks

Laura Ellis is the vice president of Data & AI at Rapid7, a prominent cybersecurity company headquartered in Boston that provides solutions for vulnerability management, threat detection and incident response. In a March 2025 interview, she discussed the potential opportunities, risks, and practical considerations for implementing AI-enabled digital human agents in the context of cybersecurity.

She contended that digital agents go well beyond simple automation, "they can provide end-to-end capabilities. For example, agents can reason about the known environment, formulate a goal, and then execute actions on it, leveraging a mix of automation and AI." In cybersecurity, this means faster and more efficient processing of massive volumes of data related to vulnerabilities, risk profiles, and threat detection.

"The potential benefits of AI agents are massive; they're able to tackle mundane human tasks at scale. But the risk is that they may execute the wrong task autonomously."

Ellis maintained that a mix of strong, knowledgeable leadership and a team of experts in ML modeling and AI engineering (data scientists and software engineering) is essential. She also stressed that teams should leverage existing, cloud-based and open-source AI agent services, wherever possible. However, she cautioned against rolling out agentic AI without the proper guardrails. Especially in sensitive areas like cybersecurity, a main concern involves when to allow digital human agents to make decisions autonomously. "The potential benefits of AI agents are massive; they're able to tackle mundane human tasks at scale," she said. "But the risk is that they may execute the wrong task autonomously." AI agents should be designed to operate autonomously in low-risk areas, while requiring human check-ins for higher-risk situations. "Start by focusing on specific, targeted goals rather than attempting to create an agent that can handle any security response."

Managing Risk

Seth Dobrin is the founder and CEO of Qantm AI, a leading AI consultancy based in Austin, Texas. Dr. Dobrin was IBM's Global Chief AI Officer, responsible for AI strategy and execution across

IBM businesses. In a recent interview, he spoke of the rapidly evolving landscape of domain-specific digital agents and the novel safety measures required for their implementation.

Dobrin pointed out that there are two primary types of AI agents. The first consists of workflows and processes integrated with LLMs like OpenAI and Anthropic. These are "relatively safe, no more risky than generative AI itself." The second type is domain-specific or task-specific AI systems representing business units, functions, or individuals. These are interesting but pose some significant AI safety challenges. "With small model agents, a human can't predict everything the AI could do," he noted, "so a human alone cannot set guardrails." He went on to say, "Humans need to define policies, and transparent/interpretable AI policing agents should enforce those policies based on the behavior of the agentic system."

For example, if a marketing AI agent were created to identify new business opportunities, humans might identify *some* possibilities involving deceptive or risky practices. However, Dobrin emphasized, "as a human, you couldn't possibly think of all the deceptive practices these AI agents could develop. So now you need some AIs around those agents to monitor what they're doing. These *policing agents* make sure these agents don't go outside policies and controls."

Ultimately, making digital human agents both safe and effective will be advantageous to developers.

Dobrin acknowledged that outcome-focused (as opposed to technology-focused) regulations and safeguards are essential, but added that regulations primarily constrain "honest people." Beyond regulation, he believes addressing the underlying development of large language models is critical, including concerns about "technological colonialism," lack of diversity, and resource allocation. Ultimately, making agents safe and effective will be advantageous to developers. "I think the startups that do this well will be the ones that get the lion's share of the marketplace," he said. "Enterprises are going to care about this."

Dobrin also notes that the rise of AI agents will require a shift in most organizations' structure and skill sets. "Everyone in the organization [will become] a manager of a set of agents."

Embracing the Digital Shift

Sandy Carter is the chief business officer and Head of Go To Market (Sales, Marketing, Communications, Community) at Unstoppable Domains, a platform for user-owned digital identity. The company recently partnered with Synergetics.ai to launch TWIN, the first blockchain-based, top-level internet domain for AI agent communication.

In a recent interview, she outlined the potential future roles that digital humans will assume—as well as the potential risks and new responsibilities to consider when adding them to the workforce.

Carter described a spectrum of AI agents, ranging from simple process executors to more sophisticated entities capable of independent work. "It could be like a junior employee, doing specifically what I asked...almost like an intern. But a more advanced agent, on its own, would consolidate my support tickets, my CRM, and my emails, and come up with insights that I probably wouldn't have come up with."

Like many other business leaders, Carter believes that AI agents hold enormous potential to revolutionize productivity, by offloading as much as 80 percent of routine tasks to digital humans. "Eventually, we're all going to be managing teams of agents. If we can give that 80 percent to an agent, we can focus on higher-impact activities, and our companies will be much better off."

The winning combination for digital human agents is to effectively combine protected private data with selected public data to use for their conclusions.

Using digital human agents is not without risk. Carter noted that, like AI itself, digital agents pose potential risks associated with data usage and provenance, potential copyright and trademark infringement issues, and inappropriate data inference. "There's a potential for data to be flowing in from ChatGPT and other unknown sources. If people base business decisions on it, just because it's 'super cool,' it could come back to bite them." The winning combination, she feels, is to effectively combine protected private data with selected, publicly available data, and using that for their conclusions.

We will all need to acquire new management skills, Carter stressed, in order to effectively handle these new, digital human team members. "Delegation is a key skill. We all need to decide which work we can delegate to an agent."

Finally, Carter noted that there are three basic requirements for building digital humans:

- **Define the outcome.** Make sure that the intended business purposes of using a digital human are clearly defined. This must include the measurable, verifiable results you plan to receive.
- **Determine the inputs.** Identify the necessary training data—both private and public—required for the agent to work effectively.
- **Establish an update frequency.** Determine how often the agent's data and its knowledgebase need to be updated. Carter explained that frequent updates are critical to maintaining a digital human's relevance and accuracy.

A Human-Centric Perspective

Denisse Goldfarb is an international speaker, author, and the CEO and founder of The People Future, a human resources consulting firm focused on digital culture, talent management, and organizational change. In addition to HR strategy consulting, she also conducts training workshops and mentors individual leaders and teams on the practical applications of digital transformation. In a recent interview, she shared her insights on the role of digital human agents in augmenting human potential.

AI in general (and digital humans in particular) represent a "superpower," going much deeper than automation, she maintained. It is about "the ability to expand our human potential by processing enormous amounts of information, learning from the collective intelligence of humanity, and accessing knowledge, ideas, products and services from anywhere in the world—instantly." In support of this, Goldfarb cited her efforts in developing AI-based digital humans that function as "intelligent career assistants." These agents are designed "not just to automate, but to amplify human potential—helping people reflect, act, and grow in a world of constant change."

For developers, Goldfarb recommends starting small and establishing "a multidisciplinary team...with a blend of software engineering, UX/UI, ethics, product development, and psychology." For teams that *use* digital human agents, she advocates that everyone develop their digital literacy and AI fluency, "understanding what AI agents can and can't do." Overall, she emphasized the importance of ***putting humans at the center*** of digital human development and use. "A digital agent should never replace empathy—it should scale it."

PRACTICAL ADVICE

Without question, creating digital humans that can eventually become ***adult***-level or even mature ***sages*** is an audacious undertaking. If these digital coworkers are to be both competent and trustworthy (like we can be, at our best), then we must apply the best of our AI technology—and the best versions of ourselves.

CHAPTER 10

A Vision for the Future

Throughout this book, we have explored the foundations, concepts, and practical methodology behind the once-fictional notion of digital human agents. These AI-enabled entities can sound, appear, and act like us. Ideally, when designed and well-implemented, they can also advance our lives and the objectives of our organizations. While they will likely never equal us in creativity or intuitive reasoning, they are certainly more efficient in the routine matters that prevent us from being more creative and intuitive.

It has been a rapid journey, from the basic technology foundations of digital humans to examples of how they can function today and the nuanced ethical considerations that must guide their development into the future. We are only beginning to know the ways they can interact with us, with digital "personas" that include the efficient *assistant*, the empathetic *companion*, and the insightful *twin*. We have also explored a methodological framework for developing these entities, progressing from the ***child*** and

adolescent stages to eventually achieving ***adult*** or even ***sage*** levels of competence and autonomy.

Digital humans are only as good (or as bad) as the training we provide them.

What once was the sole domain of science fiction is already part of our daily lives, from chatbots resolving customer queries, to virtual agents providing emotional support and connection. As we look forward, it is poised to exceed our expectations even further. For some, those expectations may be dark and pessimistic; for others, they are filled with promise. The truth is that digital human agents are only as good (or as bad) as the training we provide them—both in their competence to do things well and in their adherence to human values.

A vision for the future of digital humans must be a blend of industry observations, personal reflection, and realistic forecasts. By combining the themes of technology, experience, ethics, and societal change, this chapter will outline how digital humans could transform our world by 2030 and beyond. It will also discuss how leadership, policies, and innovation can ensure that the ***Digital Human Advantage*** truly benefits humanity.

Where We Are Today

In the mid-2020s, we are at the dawn of the digital human era. Exponential growth in AI, machine learning, big data, computing power and cloud connectivity are the technological foundations for the emergence of practical digital humans. Large language models are increasingly fluent. Natural language processing, computer vision, and advanced graphics animation have given them the ability to sound, appear, and act more like us. They greet us with friendly voices, answer our many questions, and even provide emotional support. What was once clunky and robotic is evolving into something far more natural.

Just as important today, we are grappling with the ethical implications of these technologies. Concerns about privacy, bias, and AI transparency are now mainstream topics, not just academic footnotes or obscure policy debates. Some have implemented guidelines and principles to ensure that their digital humans are worthy of our trust, and to ensure optimum transparency and data privacy. Errors and bad actors will always exist, of course, but developers are also taking measures to ensure that their digital humans' identity is secure and verifiable.

Meanwhile, real-world applications of digital humans are proliferating. In previous chapters, we observed the emergence of distinct *personas* that are sure to evolve in their involvement in our lives—and our organizations. These include the increasingly ubiquitous ***digital assistants***, from sophisticated chatbots and voice-only agents like Siri and Alexa to concierge-like AI avatars. As they become increasingly more conversational and proactive, these agents act as tireless personal or administrative aides—setting reminders, answering questions, and guiding us through processes. They also include early ***digital companions***, engaging us in personal dialogue and providing nonjudgmental listening, feedback, and even comfort at any hour. While they are currently limited in capacity, they represent a shift in how we interact with technology emotionally. Finally, they also include very early iterations of ***digital twins***, virtual replicas of ourselves. Currently, these are limited to tasks such as aggregating our calendars, notes, or even our health data, but they hold great promise as agents capable of learning our preferences, decision patterns, and communications style. In time, they may amplify our productivity and even represent us in certain contexts.

Each of these use cases involves an evolving ***digital human ecosystem***. It includes tech companies building AI and avatar platforms, enterprises integrating digital humans into their operations, and consumers engaging more frequently with AI personas. Various industries, including entertainment, healthcare, education, and even government, are exploring the use of virtual agents to increase their reach and the efficacy of their services. The mid-2020s, then, can be described as a formative period. The technology is maturing but still far from perfect. Public awareness is increasing, of both the good and bad potential, and initial norms are being established. In effect, we are building the early societal infrastructure for a world where digital human agents can become commonplace.

Trends Accelerating Change

Looking forward, there are several major trends that suggest digital humans will become more sophisticated and more integrated into our lives and businesses. Foremost of these of course is the ***advancement of artificial intelligence*** itself. As LLMs and generative AI systems go beyond Gartner's "trough of disillusionment" stage and progress to their "plateau of productivity,"[1] they will enable more fluent conversation, a deeper contextual understanding, and more realistic generation of voices and faces. We will have moved from chatbots that answer basic questions to AI agents that can hold long-term memories of interactions, exhibit a more lifelike personality, and learn continuously from each engagement.

AI advancement will also enable future digital humans to handle more complex tasks with little or no direct supervision. If an AI assistant today can draft an email or summarize a meeting, tomorrow's version may negotiate a contract or devise a project plan—in collaboration with its with human colleagues. Such progress will of course blur the lines between tool and partner.

Another relevant future trend will likely be the maturation of ***extended reality*** (XR) and ***immersive interfaces***. As VR headsets become cheaper and lighter,* and especially as AR glasses become more mainstream, it is likely that digital humans will have a greater situational presence in our offices and meeting venues. Instead of a voice on a smart device or a face on a flat screen, imagine a life-sized holographic instructor walking you through a training exercise or an AR-generated colleague sitting with you across the table. By 2030 to 2035, we may routinely interact with such digital human avatars during remote work meetings or educational seminars—perhaps even at social gatherings. This tangibility factor may make interactions more engaging and intuitive, but they also raise the stakes for how authentic and trustworthy these digital humans must be.

Increased ***connectivity*** and the ***Internet of Things*** (IoT) are major contributors to the exponential growth of digital human agents. The world is increasingly interconnected, via fiber optics, 5G cellular networks,† and satellite-based networks. For example, your digital human assistant could then move with you from place to place, interacting with smart devices, business systems, and other environments on your behalf. Such connectivity will also supply these AI personas with a rich stream of data from multiple sources—including ourselves. By leveraging data from our wearable devices, sensors, and online activities, digital humans could gain the contextual awareness needed for them to be more proactive. While this interplay of digital humans with IoT means these agents could better orchestrate our digital and physical lives, it also highlights the urgency of privacy and identity protection.

All this data handling prowess will require a massive increase in ***computer processing power***. To accomplish this, without taxing

* And less prone to creating disorientation and nausea.

† The next iteration (6G) will be deployed beginning in 2030, with significantly faster speeds and lower latency than 5G. Artificial intelligence will be integrated with 6G, enabling it to make autonomous decisions and optimize performance in real time.

our energy supply in ways that endanger the environment, breakthroughs in computer science, especially in ***quantum computing***, will be essential. In 2015, Google and NASA reported that their quantum computer solved an optimization problem 100 million times faster than a regular computer chip.[2] Others note that while conventional computers are actually faster solving ordinary problems, quantum machines excel in areas such as machine learning and cryptography.[3] In any case, quantum computation may well prove to consume less energy with greater processing power.[4] This is good news, not only for digital human agents, which be able to analyze immense datasets and solve complex problems in seconds (or less), but also for the planet we both inhabit.

On the human side of the equation, ***social acceptance and expectations*** will play a major part in the increased use of digital humans. Younger generations, those who grew up with smartphones and voice assistants, are more likely to accept digital humans as normal. Even now, millions see AI companions not as curiosities but as useful, even intimate, parts of their lives. By 2030, having an AI companion or a virtual coach could be as unremarkable as having a smartphone today. As people interact with AI-based systems more often, familiarity and acceptance will increase—***provided that such trust isn't violated by misuse***. At the same time, user expectations will increase. They will demand more natural interactions, a greater sense of empathy, and factual reliability from digital humans. As we become more comfortable working with digital humans, we will also become more dependent on them—and less tolerant of their flaws.

Finally, the ***business and economic drivers*** (such as those outlined in the Power Quadrant in Chapter 6) will continue to make AI-enabled digital humans a "must-have." Whether the primary need is efficiency, market growth, product development, or outright business model disruption, digital human agency will be the norm in 2030 and beyond. As businesses realize the need, investment in core technologies and specific applications will increase rapidly, pushing the digital human economy (by one estimate) to $125 billion by 2035.[5]

To imagine a more concrete example of the likely future, let's look at a day in the life of a typical, (albeit fictional) thirty-five-year-old professional, whom we'll call Maya. In this setting, sometime in the early 2030s, we'll look at her interaction with various digital humans throughout the day.

A Glimpse into Tomorrow

Early Morning: Maya wakes up to a familiar voice, her AI companion embodied in a smart display by her bedside. Following the opening to a favorite tune, it says, "Good morning. I noticed you didn't sleep well last night. May I adjust your schedule and set up a calming playlist for tonight?" The companion monitored her biometrics overnight—with permission—and detected some restlessness. The AI's tone expresses genuine concern, which Maya finds comforting. As she gets ready, she chats with it about the playlist, and about an upcoming family event. It listens like an old friend and offers thoughtful reminders; it never forgets birthdays or important details. Maya has never lost sight of the fact that the AI isn't a human: it's a safe, sophisticated program, but she also values its presence in her life. The companionship feels real and, in the 2030s, forming a bond with digital human agents no longer carries a social stigma—so long as she is aware of the risks.[6]

The Commute: On the drive to work, Maya still has access to her home AI companion, but it is joined by others. Her vehicle's AI doesn't have a digital human persona, per se, but it does automatically keep track of road conditions and potential driving hazards. (It can even take over and drive the car if her interactions become too distracting, but Maya usually prefers to drive the car herself.) On the way, she checks in with her company's AI office assistant, who reminds her of the day's agenda and resolves any schedule conflicts. The two digital humans are well integrated, so Maya can tell them to hold nonurgent calls and play her current audiobook—or silence—for the rest of the ride in.

The Work Routine: At 9 a.m., Maya attends an online team meeting—or, rather, her digital twin does. She works at a multinational firm, with team members in multiple time zones. She also has overlapping project commitments and simply cannot be everywhere at once. Fortunately, it's now acceptable for routine meetings or presentations to be handled by one's personal AI twin. So, while Maya focuses on a high-priority creative task, her digital twin logs into the meeting. Colleagues see a lifelike avatar of Maya, clearly identified as an AI but which also looks and sounds like her, mirroring her professional warm demeanor. Based on the real Maya's notes, her digital twin participates in the meeting, delivering updates and answering simple questions. It defers more complex questions for Maya to follow-up on later. Afterwards, the twin automatically sends Maya a summary of what transpired. Any urgent tasks are handled by the company's AI office assistant, who forwards them to her personally (and diplomatically).

This scenario, which would have seemed like pure fantasy a decade earlier, is now unremarkable. "Out of office" notices are no longer an excuse, as AI assistants and digital twins keep work moving even when humans are away.[7] Maya reviews the meeting notes and finds them thorough; her twin flagged two items for her personal attention and it handled everything else. By leveraging a digital twin, employees like Maya can be in two places at once, increasing productivity and reducing the stress from double-booked calendars. It even allows her to attend meetings where the principals (or clients) work in remote time zones.

At her actual meeting (which her twin couldn't cover because it required in person brainstorming), Maya also has the support of the company's AI project assistant. This is an enterprise-provided digital human that manages the minute details of multiple company initiatives. Appearing as a holographic facilitator at the conference room table, it helps organize ideas, fetches data upon request, and even mediates the discussion by ensuring everyone gets time to speak. And, because it knows the progress and details of other projects, it can identify and mediate potential schedule and resource conflicts.

The assistant's presence makes the meeting more efficient: It keeps track of action items and deadlines, its natural language abilities enable it to draft the meeting minutes in real time, and it can even provide translations for overseas colleagues. By the end of the meeting, everyone receives a copy of notes and a task list prepared by the AI, allowing the team to move forward swiftly. By handling the complex but mundane details well, it frees the humans on the team to focus on strategy, creativity, and relationship-building. (It goes without saying that these company AI assistants are guarded by the latest security and privacy protection measures.)

Afternoon Activities: After work, Maya swings by her elderly father's house. He lives alone, but she feels at ease knowing he isn't truly *alone:* In addition to his weekly poker buddies and a new girlfriend (all human), he has an AI companion of his own. His healthcare avatar, Sam, who has been carefully designed with the strongest possible ethical and privacy guidelines, is available to chat throughout the day. Like a friendly, older adult, he reminds Maya's father to take his medication, monitors his diet, and keeps him engaged with conversations and occasional games. In the background, Sam does keep track of her father's vital signs 24-7 but, more importantly, he provides emotional support and companionship. Her father knows that Sam is not a flesh and blood human, but that hardly diminishes the comfort he gets from the interaction.

While at her father's, Maya gets an alert via her AR glasses. Her personal digital assistant has negotiated a better rate with her father's utility company, where she has access to his account. She gets his okay and tells her assistant to switch plans. Some of Maya's friends have given their assistants permission to do such things automatically, but she prefers to keep a bit more oversight.

Afterwards, Maya has dinner with friends. Her personal and business AI agents are not turned off, but they stay strictly in the background, interrupting only when there is a real emergency. Maya's own AI companion did make the restaurant reservations, and coordinates schedules with her friends, but it always remains politely out of sight.

In the Evening: Back at home, Maya decides to unwind with a mixed reality fitness session. Her virtual trainer, a cheerful but not too gung ho 3D avatar, coaches her through yoga and strength exercises tailored to her needs. Afterwards, she consults with her personal AI companion to plan a vacation. Her digital human knows her preferences for climate and activities—as well as her budget and her schedule—and works with multiple airlines and hotels to create three possible vacation options, complete with photos and itineraries. Delighted, Maya selects one and tells her companion to book the trip.

As Maya reflects on her day, she realizes how seamlessly she interacted with various AI personas: a morning confidant, a travel companion, a work representative, a collaborative assistant, a caregiver for her father, a personal trainer, and a travel planner. Each of these was a facet of a holistic ***digital human ecosystem***, each one specializing in a role, yet also connected to her life and to all the data she needs.

For Maya, these digital humans have not diminished the importance of real human relationships or her own agency; rather, they function as a supportive entourage, amplifying what she can do in a day and enriching the quality of her life by handling the mundane or providing expertise on demand. She is careful to maintain a healthy balance, taking breaks from tech when needed and cherishing her human interactions. However, she is grateful for the advantages this digital human ecosystem provides.

The above scenario is an optimistic projection, of course. Not everyone in the 2030s will live like Maya; there will be disparities in technology access, as well as personal adoption choices. However, the purpose of this exercise is to illustrate a ***potential***, ***hopeful*** future, given the current trends and trajectories. It shows digital humans functioning in harmony as companions, twins, and assistants, delivering convenience, emotional support, enhanced productivity, personalized experiences, and other tangible benefits. These represent the promise of the Digital Human Advantage—the idea that integrating digital human agents into our lives can ***amplify human potential***, drive productivity, and improve well-being.

This future vision must be tempered with realism, however. To move forward, we must also acknowledge the challenges and pitfalls that accompany such a world. To guide digital humans well, we must examine what could go wrong, and then guide them deliberately toward the best-case outcomes.

Balancing On the Edge: Opportunities and Challenges

Maya's bright future will not unfold smoothly or by default. Digital humans, like any other powerful technology, come with very real risks. To overcome them requires foresight, good design, and exceptional management.

Ethical Use and the Potential for Misuse. As digital humans become more lifelike, the potential for misuse grows, including manipulation and deception by malicious actors. They could use advanced AI avatars to impersonate real people (so-called deepfakes) and deceive others. We have already seen early cases of this, including digital imposters on video calls who have tricked people into large financial transfers by perfectly mimicking trusted individuals.[8] By 2030, if everyone has a digital twin, then digitally verifying their identity, while difficult, will be crucial.

The counter to this problem is the ethical design principle of ***transparency***. Digital humans should never be designed to fool people into thinking that they are human.[9] They should willingly identify as AI and leave perceptible "tells" when needed. Failing to do so undermines trust. Our vision for 2030 assumes that we implement strong measures, both technical and legal, to distinguish and control AI-generated content, so that digital humans become trusted collaborators, not a source of pervasive scams or misinformation.

Bias. Another challenge is the need to ensure that digital humans act fairly and without prejudice. All AI-based systems learn from data, some of which may contain historical bias or a lack of diversity. This could easily but inadvertently perpetuate stereotypes or discrimination if not carefully managed. For example, an AI assistant used in hiring or customer service must be monitored, especially early on, so that it doesn't give preferential treatment or insensitive responses based on gender, race, or accent.

This well-known issue affecting AI in general must be mitigated through the use of more diverse training data, bias detection audits, and the inclusion of ethicists in development teams. It is also imperative to design digital humans that ***respect all users***. This is a practical matter, not just a moral obligation. An offensive AI will not be tolerated, especially when a competitor's unbiased digital human becomes more popular. The ideal digital human ecosystem benefits *everyone*, not just certain groups. It is in the public interest for AI companions to be adept at understanding cultural differences, for AI assistants to be accessible to people with disabilities, and for digital twins to represent their users accurately and fairly.

Privacy and Data Security. Digital humans thrive on data. The more they know about us, the better they can serve us. But this raises significant privacy concerns. Your future digital companion's deep profile might include your health metrics, your daily schedule, your likes and dislikes, and even the content of your messages. Protecting this sensitive personal data is paramount. In our envisioned future, ***privacy by design*** is a core principle. Digital humans will only collect data with user consent and only what is necessary.[10]

Data must be stored securely and in a decentralized or encrypted form that even service providers cannot easily abuse. Users must always have clear control—able to see what their AI knows about them and delete or hide information at will. Stronger data protection laws and regulations (built on frameworks like the European Union's GDPR) will likely be in place by then, with hefty penalties for companies that fail to safeguard user data.

The trust that people place in their digital humans will depend on rigorous privacy protection. After all, in our future scenario, one of the reasons that Maya trusts her assistant to negotiate a bill is the confidence that her financial data won't leak or be exploited.

Dependency and Human Skills. An often-understated risk of relying on digital humans is how they might affect human behavior and skills. If AI assistants do so much for us—from remembering things to making decisions—we might see an atrophy of certain abilities. For example, if we rely on so-called companions who always agree with us and praise our every word, we are likely to do poorly in normal social situations, and especially in handling disagreements. If we over rely on assistants for tasks we just don't want to do, our ability to learn and grow may suffer.

By 2030, we will need to have strategies in place to prevent negative cognitive or social effects. This includes designing AI to *augment* rather than replace human effort. For example, an educational AI tutor would be designed to cultivate students' problem-solving abilities, not simply provide the answers.

In our optimistic future, we need a clearly defined "wellness practice" for AI. In this model, digital humans ***enhance*** human skills by taking care of routine tasks and providing coaching, while at the same time we deliberately practice and value human skills that are unique and not replicable by AI. These include creativity, empathy, critical thinking, hands-on craftsmanship, and the joy of face-to-face relationships. Indeed, if used well, freeing humans from drudgery can spark a renaissance of human creativity and interpersonal connection, as people reclaim time to spend with each other or pursue their passions.

Job Disruption and Economic Impact. The rise of digital humans will inevitably disrupt job markets. Routine communication and information delivery roles will be partly or fully taken over by AI avatars and agents. As with past automations in manufacturing, this will require careful management—especially since it affects white-collar workers for the first time. Using more AI-enabled digital employees will lead to job displacement, but it will also create new roles and opportunities. Entirely new professions are likely to emerge, but our responsibility is to ensure a just transition. That means using upskilling and reskilling programs to prepare the workforce for jobs that leverage AI. However, it also means strengthening social safety nets to help those who do lose work to automation.

Historically, technology has always been a net job creator in the long run, but the transition can be painful. Ideally, the Digital Human Advantage should augment human workers, not replace them outright. Maya's AI aides made her more productive but did not replace her. Organizations should focus on using digital humans to boost human productivity and reach, not merely cut labor costs. With enlightened leadership, the workforce of the future can be one where humans and AI teammates each do what they do best.

Guiding Digital Humans Responsibly

To ensure that digital humans act responsibly—and avoid the many pitfalls described earlier—will require ***leadership***, not just from top executives or heads of government, but from all levels of technology and business, including end users. We all have a role in shaping the norms and rules affecting digital humans and the ways we work with them. This involves five specific domains:

Sound Business Principles. Companies driving AI and digital human development carry a great responsibility, no matter where they fall in the Power Quadrant. Visionary leaders in this space look beyond short-term gains and focus on long-term trust and value. This means prioritizing ethics and user well-being as part of the product strategy, not as an afterthought. For example, a company releasing an AI companion should set boundaries so that it does not exploit users' emotions or attention in unhealthy ways. Business leaders should champion AI ***transparency*** and commit to developing AI solutions using ***interdisciplinary teams***. This means including psychologists, sociologists, and ethicists working alongside engineers and data scientists—to better foresee how their AI might impact different users.

Leaders like these can set industry standards by publishing their principles and best practices, and by being transparent about both the capabilities and the shortcomings of their digital humans. Moreover, forward-thinking companies will collaborate to create industry-wide ethical frameworks—much like the way medical ethics guide healthcare—maintaining a "do no harm" baseline. There is a competitive advantage as well. Users will gravitate towards brands that they trust. In the future, a hallmark of successful digital human products may be an earned reputation for safety, privacy, and fairness.

Policy and Regulation. In the long run, governments and international bodies must be proactive in establishing regulations that keep pace with AI innovation. If left purely to market forces, and without an impartial referee, the drive for profit could overpower social considerations. We are already seeing movement in this direction. By the late 2020s, there will be clearer rules in areas such as: requiring public-facing AI systems to pass basic safety and bias tests, mandating user consent and data protection for AI services, and perhaps even licensing or auditing of advanced AI, similar to the way we regulate medicine or aviation in the interest of public safety.

As public awareness of AI's potential grows, there will likely be more laws against impersonation and fraud, making it illegal to create or use a digital human of someone without authorization. Policymakers should also consider the concept of an ***AI accountability framework***. If an autonomous digital agent causes harm, who is liable—the user, the developer, or the AI itself? Clarifying this matter will incentivize proper oversight.

The challenge is of course to craft smart regulations that ***protect people without stifling innovation***. This will require ongoing dialogue between regulators, technologists, and civil society. International cooperation will be important too, since digital interactions cross borders by definition. By 2030, perhaps we will see something akin to a "Geneva Convention" for AI, a set of global norms on the use of AI and digital humans. For example, they might forbid autonomous AI weapons or the manipulation and exploitation of vulnerable populations with AI. Such measures may sound ambitious, but they are becoming increasingly necessary as AI's influence grows.

Innovation With Purpose. The engineering and research community has a pivotal role in solving the technical challenges related to ethics and efficacy. Innovations are needed to make digital humans not only more capable, but also more trustworthy. One key area is ***AI explainability***—developing AI systems whose decisions and actions can be understood and traced by humans. This would help in auditing AI behavior for bias or errors. Another is ***AI safety***—techniques to ensure that AI agents stay within intended bounds and can gracefully handle unexpected situations or ambiguous instructions without malfunctioning. For digital humans that learn and operate continuously, having robust fail-safes will be critical. These would be like an emergency off switch or an ethics module that overrides questionable actions. Innovators also need to work on ***AI standards for interoperability***. By 2030, individuals might use digital human services from different providers, just as we use different applications and operating systems today. Ensuring that these AI systems can work together and share data securely (with user permission) will create a smoother ecosystem.

Crucially, technical innovation must also focus on inclusivity. For example, improving natural language understanding for different dialects and languages will ensure that these AI-enabled digital humans serve a global, diverse user base, without bias. We also need far more research, sociological and psychological, on how people relate to digital humans over long periods. Such knowledge can inform better design that enhances positive outcomes (such as improved mental health or productivity) and avoids negative ones (such as dependency or confusion between AI and real humans). When technologists innovate with these goals in mind, they push the field toward more human-centric solutions.

Education and Digital Literacy. As digital humans become more common, education also must evolve so that everyone can navigate in an AI-rich world. This starts in schools by including AI in curricula—not just how to code, but how AI works, its strengths and limitations, and its ethical implications. By 2030, understanding AI may be as fundamental as understanding electricity or the internet is today. People should learn how to critically evaluate the output of an AI assistant, how to tell when a digital video might be fake, and how to use digital twins responsibly.

Beyond formal education, public awareness campaigns and community discussions will help normalize these technologies and demystify them. The more society understands AI, the more effectively we can cocreate norms for its use. For instance, if everyone knows that an AI companion might show *apparent* empathy but doesn't truly "feel," then users can keep their relationships with these companions in perspective. If consumers are savvy about their data rights, then they will demand better privacy controls from providers. Empowering users through knowledge is a form of bottom-up leadership that is just as important as top-down policy. A digitally literate society is less likely to be manipulated by bad actors and more likely to reap the benefits of digital humans with open eyes.

Multi-Stakeholder Collaboration. No single entity can solve all these challenges or realize this vision alone. There must be collaboration across industries and disciplines. Thankfully, we already see partnerships forming—tech companies working with nonprofits on AI ethics, governments consulting academia for policy advice, and international alliances on AI research. These must continue and broaden. For example, a coalition between healthcare providers, patient advocates, AI developers, and regulators could establish guidelines for using digital humans in mental health therapy, making sure efficacy and privacy standards are met. Or, a consortium of corporations could pool resources to develop open-source tools for detecting deepfakes, which would benefit society as a whole.

Collaboration also means listening to the voices of those most affected. This includes inclusion of diverse perspectives—different ages, cultures, and socioeconomic backgrounds—in designing a digital human future that serves everyone. By 2030, one could envision the creation of a "Digital Human Council" or similar body, comprised of ethicists, technologists, user representatives, and lawmakers. Such a body would meet regularly to assess the state of digital humans and advise on emerging issues. While that may sound idealistic, structures like these can provide continuous guidance as the technology evolves.

Guiding digital humans responsibly requires a concerted effort on multiple fronts. It is a socio-technical endeavor: Technology shapes society, and society must shape the technology. With enlightened leadership in business and government, purposeful innovation, and an informed public, we can build a framework where digital humans are developed and deployed in alignment with core human values.

The late 2020s will be remembered either as the time we set the right course for the digital human era, or when we failed to put guardrails on and allowed the technology to careen into problems. I am optimistic that we will choose the better path.

Embracing the Digital Human Advantage

As we face the future, one thing is clear: AI-enabled digital humans are poised to become an integral part of how we live, work, and relate to one another. This transformation will bring tremendous opportunities to augment human capabilities. It also imposes significant responsibilities to ensure these tools align with our ethical and social priorities. This chapter paints a vision for the future that is hopeful and yet mindful of the hurdles we face. It is a future where technology enriches human life, where digital humans can help unlock human potential and drive progress—so long as we guide its values and its destiny.

Realizing this vision will not happen on its own. It calls for action from all of us who have a stake in the future:

- ***Business Leaders:*** If you are an executive or entrepreneur, how you adopt AI today will shape society (and your organization) tomorrow. Use the Digital Human Advantage to complement and empower your workforce and customers, not to exploit them. Champion ethical AI practices in your organization. Alongside revenue and productivity, make fairness, transparency, and user well-being your key performance indicators. Invest in your people: train them to work effectively with AI and elevate them to higher-value roles as automation takes over routine tasks. By leading with foresight and integrity, you not only avoid backlash, but also build trust that becomes a competitive edge in the AI age.

- ***Technologists and Innovators:*** To the engineers, data scientists, designers, and researchers, keep pushing the boundaries of what AI can do, but always ask *should* we do it, not just *can* we do it. Embed ethics into every step of development. Engage with experts in other fields to understand the human context of your work. Strive to create digital humans that are not just smarter, but also wiser in how they interact with people. Your innovations should emphasize privacy, security, and inclusivity as much as efficiency or realism. Remember that every line of code in an AI system can affect a life. Code with empathy for the end user. And be transparent about AI's limits; manage expectations so users can use it appropriately. By innovating responsibly, you ensure that technology remains a servant to humanity's needs and values.
- ***Policymakers and Society in General:*** For lawmakers, educators, and indeed all citizens, engage actively in the conversation about our AI-driven future. We need thoughtful regulations that safeguard rights and safety without impeding beneficial innovation. Support policies that promote AI literacy, workforce transition, and research into AI's societal impacts. As individuals, approach digital humans with an open mind but also healthy skepticism. Demand clarity about how AI systems use your data and affect your life. Cultivate your own "digital wisdom:" know when to rely on your AI helper and when to seek a

human touch. By voicing your expectations and concerns, you guide both companies and governments to make better decisions. Ultimately, society must decide what role we want digital humans to play, and that decision comes from millions of small choices and voices, including yours.

The rise of digital humans represents a new chapter in the story of technology and humanity. It is a story of convergence, where our digital creations become more humanlike, and we humans become more interwoven with digital experiences. If we succeed in guiding this journey well, the year 2030 and beyond will not be a dystopia of isolation or a cold, machine-dominated world; instead, it will be a time of augmented humanity. It will be a time when digital humans amplify the best parts of us. They will enhance our creativity, our empathy, our productivity, and our capacity to connect. The optimistic scenario in this chapter show how life could flourish when AI is integrated thoughtfully—families supported, workers empowered, learners inspired, and communities served in new and personalized ways.

These outcomes are far from guaranteed. They require that we be vigilant and proactive now. Consider this as a call to action: The Digital Human Advantage is not just an advantage for businesses or technology; it can become an advantage for humanity. It begins today. Let's get to work.

Endnotes

Introduction

1 Hope Reese, "Why Microsoft's 'Tay' AI bot went wrong," *TechRepublic*, published March 24, 2016, https://www.techrepublic.com/article/why-microsofts-tay-ai-bot-went-wrong/.

Chapter 1

1 Asha Saxena, *The AI Factor: How to Apply Artificial Intelligence and Use Big Data to Grow Your Business Exponentially*, (Post Hill Press, 2023), pp. 15–17.

2 Gil Press, "AI Stats News: 86% Of Consumers Prefer Humans To Chatbots," *Forbes*, updated December 15, 2019, https://www.forbes.com/sites/gilpress/2019/10/02/ai-stats-news-86-of-consumers-prefer-to-interact-with-a-human-agent-rather-than-a-chatbot/.

3 Jake Rossen, "The Tragic Life of Clippy, the World's Most Hated Virtual Assistant," *Mental Floss*, published July 31, 2023, https://www.mentalfloss.com/article/504767/tragic-life-clippy-worlds-most-hated-virtual-assistant.

4 Simran Kaur and Richa Sharma, "Emotion AI: Integrating Emotional Intelligence with Artificial Intelligence in the Digital Workplace," *Advances in Science, Technology & Innovation* (2021): 337–43, https://doi.org/10.1007/978-3-030-66218-9_39.

5 Lisa Feldman Barrett, Ralph Adolphs, Stacy Marsella, Aleix M. Martinez, and Seth D. Pollak, "Emotional Expressions Reconsidered: Challenges to Inferring Emotion from Human Facial Movements," *Psychological Science in the Public Interest* 20, no. 1 (July 2019): 1–68, https://doi.org/10.1177/1529100619832930.

6 Shensheng Wang,, Scott O. Lilienfeld, and Philippe Rochat, "The Uncanny Valley: Existence and Explanations," *Review of General Psychology* 19, no. 4 (December 2015): 393–407, https://doi.org/10.1037/gpr0000056.

7 Tae Woo Kim, Li Jiang, Adam Duhachek, Hyejin Lee, and Aaron Garvey, "Do You Mind If I Ask You a Personal Question? How AI Service Agents Alter Consumer Self-Disclosure," *Journal of Service Research* 25, no. 4 (August 18, 2022): 649–66, https://doi.org/10.1177/10946705221120232.

8 Patrick R. Laughlin, Erin C. Hatch, Jonathan S. Silver and Lee Boh, "Groups perform better than the best individuals on letters-to-numbers problems: Effects of group size.," *Journal of Personality and Social Psychology* 90, no. 4 (April 2006): 644–51, https://doi.org/10.1037/0022-3514.90.4.644.

9 Abdullah Almaatouq, Mohammed Alsobay, Ming Yin, and Duncan J. Watts, "Task complexity moderates group synergy," *Proceedings of the National Academy of Sciences* 118, no. 36 (September 7, 2021), https://doi.org/10.1073/pnas.2101062118.

10 Jalal Hanaysha and Putri Rozita Tahir, "Examining the Effects of Employee Empowerment, Teamwork, and Employee Training on Job Satisfaction," *Procedia - Social and Behavioral Sciences* 219 (May 2016): 272–82, https://doi.org/10.1016/j.sbspro.2016.05.016.

Chapter 2

1 Mahmut Özer, "Is Artificial Intelligence Hallucinating?," *Turkish Journal of Psychiatry* 35, no. 4 (October 14, 2024), https://doi.org/10.5080/u27587.

2 Cem Dilmegani, "When Will AGI/Singularity Happen? 8,590 Predictions Analyzed," *AIMultiple Research*, updated August 1, 2025, https://research.aimultiple.com/artificial-general-intelligence-singularity-timing/.

3 Gustavo Assunção, Bruno Patrão, Miguel Castelo-Branco, and Paulo Menezes, "An Overview of Emotion in Artificial Intelligence," *IEEE Transactions on Artificial Intelligence* 3, no. 6 (December 2022): 867–86, https://doi.org/10.1109/tai.2022.3159614.

4 Mike Seymour, Lingyao (Ivy) Yuan, Alan Dennis, and Kai Riemer, "Have We Crossed the Uncanny Valley? Understanding Affinity, Trustworthiness, and Preference for Realistic Digital Humans in Immersive Environments," *Journal of the Association for Information Systems* 22, no. 3 (2021): 591–617, https://doi.org/10.17705/1jais.00674.

5 Mike Seymour, Lingyao (Ivy) Yuan, Alan R. Dennis, and Kai Riemer, "Less Artificial, More Intelligent: Understanding Affinity, Trustworthiness, and Preference for Digital Humans," *Information Systems Research* 36, no. 4 (September 2, 2024), https://doi.org/10.1287/isre.2022.0203.

6 Partha Pratim Ray, "Web3: A comprehensive review on background, technologies, applications, zero-trust architectures, challenges and future directions," *Internet of Things and Cyber-Physical Systems* 3 (2023): 213–48, https://doi.org/10.1016/j.iotcps.2023.05.003.

7 MIT Technology Review Editors, "Explainer: What is a blockchain?," *MIT Technology Review*, published April 23, 2018, https://www.technologyreview.com/2018/04/23/143477/explainer-what-is-a-blockchain/.

8 Rebecca Liao, "Web3 Is The Home For Autonomous Consumer AI Agents," *Forbes*, published March 31, 2025, https://www.forbes.com/councils/forbestechcouncil/2025/03/31/web3-is-the-home-for-autonomous-consumer-ai-agents/.

ENDNOTES

Chapter 3

1 Emma Rumney, "British bank RBS hires 'digital human' Cora on probation," *Reuters*, updated February 21, 2018, https://www.reuters.com/article/technology/british-bank-rbs-hires-digital-human-cora-on-probation-idUSKCN1G523J/.

2 Lisa Joyce, "Android Tellers in Branches: Cool or Creepy?," *The Financial Brand*, published February 27, 2018, https://thefinancialbrand.com/news/banking-technology/android-human-robot-digital-banking-experience-70651.

3 Mark Samuels, "How Gen AI means better customer experiences - see one bank's approach," *ZDNET*, published February 1, 2025, https://www.zdnet.com/article/how-gen-ai-means-better-customer-experiences-see-one-banks-approach/.

4 Mike Seymour, Dan Lovallo, Kai Riemer, Alan R. Dennis, and Lingyao (Ivy) Yuan, "AI With a Human Face," *Harvard Business Review*, March-April 2023, https://hbr.org/2023/03/ai-with-a-human-face.

5 Conn Hastings, "Virtual humans can identify post-traumatic stress in soldiers," *Frontiers in Science* News, published October 12, 2017, https://www.frontiersin.org/news/2017/10/12/virtual-humans-post-traumatic-stress-frontiers-in-robotics-and-ai/.

6 Rachel Cramer, "Are digital humans the employees of the future?," *Iowa State University News Service*, published February 20, 2023, https://www.news.iastate.edu/news/are-digital-humans-employees-future.

7 Michael D. Smith, "Masters of None: The Flawed Logic of One-Size-Fits-All Education," *The MIT Press Reader*, published March 3, 2025, https://thereader.mitpress.mit.edu/masters-of-none-the-flawed-logic-of-one-size-fits-all-education/.

8 Shudong Yang, Huiyi Tian, Lin Sun, and Xueying Yu, "From One-size-fits-all Teaching to Adaptive Learning: The Crisis and Solution of Education in the Era of AI," *Journal of Physics: Conference Series* 1237, no. 4 (June 2019): 042039, https://doi.org/10.1088/1742-6596/1237/4/042039.

9 Ashok Manoharan, "Next-Gen Education: 8 Strategies Leveraging AI in Learning Platforms," *Forbes*, published June 4, 2024, https://www.forbes.com/councils/forbestechcouncil/2024/06/04/next-gen-education-8-strategies-leveraging-ai-in-learning-platforms/.

10 Huanhuan Wang, Ahmed Tlili, Ronghuai Huang, Zhenyu Cai, Min Li, Zui Cheng, Dong Yang, Mengti Li, Xixian Zhu, and Cheng Fei, "Examining the applications of intelligent tutoring systems in real educational contexts: A systematic literature review from the social experiment perspective," *Education and Information Technologies* 28, no. 7 (January 7, 2023): 9113–48, https://doi.org/10.1007/s10639-022-11555-x.

11 George Vlahakis, "Meet your new AI colleague; Kelley professor studies working with digital humans," Kelley School of Business, published February 15, 2023, https://blog.kelley.iu.edu/2023/02/15/meet-your-new-ai-colleague-kelley-professor-studies-working-with-digital-humans/.

Chapter 4

1 Klaudia Jaźwińska and Aisvarya Chandrasekar, "AI Search Has a Citation Problem," *Columbia Journalism Review*, published March 6, 2025, https://www.cjr.org/tow_center/we-compared-eight-ai-search-engines-theyre-all-bad-at-citing-news.php.

2 Bernard Marr, "Generative AI Vs. Agentic AI: The Key Differences Everyone Needs to Know," *Forbes*, published February 3, 2025, https://www.forbes.com/sites/bernardmarr/2025/02/03/generative-ai-vs-agentic-ai-the-key-differences-everyone-needs-to-know/.

3 *Britannica*, "Ecosystem," last updated August 4, 2025, https://www.britannica.com/science/ecosystem.

4 Roy T. Fielding and Richard N. Taylor, "Principled design of the modern Web architecture," *ISCE'00: Proceedings of the 22nd international conference on Software engineering'* (June 1, 2000): 407–16, https://doi.org/10.1145/337180.337228.

5 "BofA's Erica Surpasses 2 Billion Interactions, Helping 42 Million Clients since Launch." Bank of America. August 20, 2025. https://newsroom.bankofamerica.com/content/newsroom/press-releases/2024/04/bofa-s-erica-surpasses-2-billion-interactions--helping-42-millio.html.

6 "The Inside Story of Getting Boston Dynamics' Robots To Dance For Viral Video," *CBS News*, published January 21, 2021, https://www.cbsnews.com/boston/news/dancing-robots-video-boston-dynamics-waltham-massachusetts-marc-raibert/.

7 Lauren Leffer, "AI Chatbots Will Never Stop Hallucinating," *Scientific American*, published April 5, 2024, https://www.scientificamerican.com/article/chatbot-hallucinations-inevitable/.

8 Juan Carlos Nieves, Mauricio Osorio, David Rojas-Velazquez, Yazmín Magallanes, and Andreas Brännström, "Digital Companions for Well-being: Challenges and Opportunities," *Journal of Intelligent & Fuzzy Systems: Applications in Engineering and Technology* (March 25, 2024): 1–11, https://doi.org/10.3233/jifs-219336.

9 Rohit Kaul, Chinedu Ossai, Abdur Rahim Mohammad Forkan, Prem Prakash Jayaraman, John Zelcer, Stephen Vaughn, and Nilmini Wickramasinghe, "The role of AI for developing digital twins in healthcare: The case of cancer care," *WIREs Data Mining and Knowledge Discovery* 13, no. 1 (November 21, 2022), https://doi.org/10.1002/widm.1480.

10 Eric Schmidt and Craig Mundie, "We Need to Figure Out How to Coevolve with AI," *Time*, published November 21, 2024, https://time.com/7177929/eric-schmidt-craig-mundie-essay-coevolve-with-ai/.

Chapter 5

1 Haleluya Hadero, "Artificial intelligence, real emotion. People are seeking a romantic connection with the perfect bot," *AP News*, updated February 14, 2024, https://apnews.com/article/ai-girlfriend-boyfriend-replika-paradot-113df1b9ed069ed56162793b50f3a9fa.

ENDNOTES

2 Jessica Grose, "Opinion | Say Goodbye to Your Kid's Imaginary Friend," *The New York Times*, published April 16, 2025, https://www.nytimes.com/2025/04/16/opinion/teens-chatbot-threat.html.

3 Bethanie Maples, Merve Cerit, Aditya Vishwanath, and Roy Pea, "Loneliness and suicide mitigation for students using GPT3-enabled chatbots," *npj Mental Health Research* 3 (January 22, 2024), https://doi.org/10.1038/s44184-023-00047-6.

4 Bobby Allyn, "Deepfake video of Zelenskyy could be 'tip of the iceberg' in info war, experts warn," *NPR*, uploaded March 16, 2022, https://www.npr.org/2022/03/16/1087062648/deepfake-video-zelenskyy-experts-war-manipulation-ukraine-russia.

5 Nick Robins-Early, "CEO of world's biggest ad firm targeted by deepfake scam," *The Guardian*, published May 10, 2024, https://www.theguardian.com/technology/article/2024/may/10/ceo-wpp-deepfake-scam.

6 Lucas Whittaker, Kate Letheren, and Rory Mulcahy, "The Rise of Deepfakes: A Conceptual Framework and Research Agenda for Marketing," *Australasian Marketing Journal* 29, no. 3 (March 16, 2021): 204–14, https://doi.org/10.1177/1839334921999479.

7 Jen Caltrider, Misha Rykov, and Zoë MacDonald, "Romantic AI Chatbots Don't Have Your Privacy at Heart," Mozilla Foundation, published February 14, 2024, https://www.mozillafoundation.org/en/privacynotincluded/articles/happy-valentines-day-romantic-ai-chatbots-dont-have-your-privacy-at-heart/.

8 Sam Wolfson, "Amazon's Alexa recorded private conversation and sent it to random contact," *The Guardian*, published May 24, 2018, https://www.theguardian.com/technology/2018/may/24/amazon-alexa-recorded-conversation.

9 Max Zahn, "Collection of voice data for profit raises privacy fears," *ABC News*, published January 18, 2023, https://abcnews.go.com/Technology/collection-voice-data-profit-raises-privacy-fears/story?id=96363792.

10 Valentin Hofmann, Pratyusha Ria Kalluri, Dan Jurafsky, and Sharese King, "AI generates covertly racist decisions about people based on their dialect," *Nature* 633 (August 28, 2024): 147–54, https://doi.org/10.1038/s41586-024-07856-5.

11 Abdullah Hussein Sham, Kadir Aktas, Davit Rizhinashvili, Danila Kuklianov, Fatih Alisinanoglu, Ikechukwu Ofodile, Cagri Ozcinar, and Gholamreza Anbarjafari, "Ethical AI in facial expression analysis: racial bias," *Signal, Image and Video Processing* 17 (May 9, 2022): 399–406, https://doi.org/10.1007/s11760-022-02246-8.

12 Mark West, Rebecca Kraut, and Chew Han Ei, "I'd blush if I could: closing gender divides in digital skills through education," UNESCO (2019), https://doi.org/10.54675/rapc9356.

13 "OECD AI Principles Overview," Organisation for Economic Co-operation and Development, accessed April 19, 2025, https://oecd.ai/en/ai-principles.

14 "AI-generated news presenter appears in Kuwait," *Al Jazeera*, published April 10, 2023, https://www.aljazeera.com/news/2023/4/10/ai-generated-news-presenter-appears-in-kuwait.

15 Katz, Leslie. "This AI-Generated Influencer Can Pull in Almost $11,000 a Month." *Forbes*, February 20, 2024. https://www.forbes.com/sites/lesliekatz/2023/11/24/this-ai-generated-influencer-can-pull-in-10000-euros-a-month/.

16 Mrinmay Dey, "IBM to pause hiring in plan to replace 7,800 jobs with AI - Bloomberg News," *Yahoo! News*, updated May 1, 2023, https://ca.finance.yahoo.com/news/ibm-pause-hiring-plans-replace-212747083.html.

17 Karim Lakhani, "AI Won't Replace Humans—But Humans With AI Will Replace Humans Without AI," *Harvard Business Review*, published August 4, 2023, https://hbr.org/2023/08/ai-wont-replace-humans-but-humans-with-ai-will-replace-humans-without-ai.

18 "High-level summary of the AI Act," EU Artificial Intelligence Act, updated May 30, 2024, https://artificialintelligenceact.eu/high-level-summary/.

19 Greg Satell and Yassmin Abdel-Magied, "AI Fairness Isn't Just an Ethical Issue," *Harvard Business Review*, published October 20, 2020, https://hbr.org/2020/10/ai-fairness-isnt-just-an-ethical-issue.

20 Neil Postman, *Technopoly: The Surrender of Culture to Technology* (Alfred A. Knopf, 1992), p. 9.

Chapter 6

1 Sameer Kumar and Ralph Harms, "Improving business processes for increased operational efficiency: a case study," *Journal of Manufacturing Technology Management* 15, no. 7 (October 1, 2004): 662–74, https://doi.org/10.1108/17410380410555907.

2 Murray Weidenbaum, "Outsourcing: Pros and cons," *Business Horizons* 48, no. 4 (July–August 2005): 311–15, https://doi.org/10.1016/j.bushor.2004.11.001.

3 Mohd Fitri Mansor, Noor Hidayah Abu, Aida Nazima Abashah, and Muhammad Asyraf Mohd Kassim, "Cost Reduction and Business Strategy Matters to Human Resource Outsourcing? A Validation by HR Experts from Government Link Companies (GLC's)," *MATEC Web of Conferences* 150 (February 23, 2018): 05033, https://doi.org/10.1051/matecconf/201815005033.

4 Tania Chanda, "Public Perception of AI-Generated Chatbot in Public Relations: Trust, Satisfaction, and Commitment," (master's thesis, University of Dayton, May 2024), https://etd.ohiolink.edu/acprod/odb_etd/ws/send_file/send?accession=dayton171473716269485&disposition=inline.

5 Yu-Shan (Sandy) Huang and Paula Dootson, "Chatbots and service failure: When does it lead to customer aggression," *Journal of Retailing and Consumer Services* 68 (September 2022): 103044, https://doi.org/10.1016/j.jretconser.2022.103044.

6 Jim C. Collins, *Good to Great: Why Some Companies Make the Leap... and Others Don't* (Harper Business, 2001).

7 Joanna Bryson and Alan Winfield, "Standardizing Ethical Design for Artificial Intelligence and Autonomous Systems," *Computer* 50, no. 5 (May 2017): 116–19, https://doi.org/10.1109/mc.2017.154.

8 James Manyika and Kevin Sneader, "AI, automation, and the future of work: Ten things to solve for," *McKinsey & Company*, published June 1, 2018, https://www.mckinsey.com/featured-insights/future-of-work/ai-automation-and-the-future-of-work-ten-things-to-solve-for.

ENDNOTES

Chapter 7

1 Sidney Fussell, "Alexa Wants to Know How You're Feeling Today," *The Atlantic*, published October 12, 2018, https://www.theatlantic.com/technology/archive/2018/10/alexa-emotion-detection-ai-surveillance/572884/.

2 Nicholas Epley, "A Mind like Mine: The Exceptionally Ordinary Underpinnings of Anthropomorphism," *Journal of the Association for Consumer Research* 3, no. 4 (October 2018): 591–98, https://doi.org/10.1086/699516.

3 Jessica McFadyen, Johanna Habicht, Larisa-Maria Dina, Ross Harper, Tobias U. Hauser, and Max Rollwage, "AI-enabled conversational agent increases engagement with cognitive-behavioral therapy: A randomized controlled trial," *medRxiv*, November 2, 2024, https://doi.org/10.1101/2024.11.01.24316565.

4 Shuhei Imamura, Yoko Gozu, Moe Tsutsumi, Kaname Hayashi, Chiaki Mori, Megumi Ishikawa, Megumi Takada, Tomotaka Ogiso, Keiko Suzuki, Shota Okabe, Takefumi Kikusui, and Kentaro Kajiya, "Higher oxytocin concentrations occur in subjects who build affiliative relationships with companion robots," *iScience* 26, no. 12 (December 2023): 108562, https://doi.org/10.1016/j.isci.2023.108562.

5 "Digital Human Market Size & Share Analysis - Growth Trends & Forecasts (2025–2030)," *Mordor Intelligence*, accessed May 7, 2025, https://www.mordorintelligence.com/industry-reports/digital-human-market#:~:text=The%20digital%20human%20market%20stands,%2C%20reflecting%20a%2035.21%25%20CAGR.

6 "About Emma," City of Amarillo, accessed March 19, 2025, https://www.amarillo.gov/about-emma/.

7 Ying Qu, Chris K. Y. Lo, and Eunsoo Baek, "From Humanoid to Virtual Humans: A Systematic Literature Review of Avatar Marketing," *International Journal of Human–Computer Interaction* (April 2, 2025): 1–20, https://doi.org/10.1080/10447318.2025.2464889.

8 Emily Rose McRae, et al., "Hype Cycle for Workforce Transformation, 2024," *Gartner Research*, July 18, 2024, https://www.scribd.com/document/819728442/Hype-Cycle-for-the-Future-of-Work-2024.

9 Shieber, Jonathan. "The Makers of the Virtual Influencer, Lil Miquela, Snag Real Money from Silicon Valley." *TechCrunch*, April 24, 2018. https://techcrunch.com/2018/04/23/the-makers-of-the-virtual-influencer-lil-miquela-snag-real-money-from-silicon-valley/.

10 Gretchen Oestreicher, "Virtual & AI Influencers in 2025," Metricool, published April 30, 2025, https://metricool.com/ai-virtual-influencers/#:~:text=In%202025%2C%20we're%20seeing,ever%20picking%20up%20a%20phone.

11 Erik Cambria, Soujanya Poria, Amir Hussain, and Bing Liu, "Computational Intelligence for Affective Computing and Sentiment Analysis [Guest Editorial]," *IEEE Computational Intelligence Magazine* 14, no. 2 (May 2019): 16–17, https://doi.org/10.1109/mci.2019.2901082.

12 Li Zhou, Jianfeng Gao, Di Li, and Heung-Yeung Shum, "The Design and Implementation of XiaoIce, an Empathetic Social Chatbot," *Computational Linguistics* 46, no. 1 (March 2020): 53–93, https://doi.org/10.1162/coli_a_00368.

13 Eve, "Woebot–the bleeding intelligent self-help therapist and companion," HBS Digital Innovation and Transformation, updated April 21, 2020, https://d3.harvard.edu/platform-digit/submission/woebot-the-bleeding-intelligent-self-help-therapist-and-companion/.

14 Alison Darcy, Jade Daniels, David Salinger, Paul Wicks, and Athena Robinson, "Evidence of Human-Level Bonds Established with a Digital Conversational Agent: Cross-sectional, Retrospective Observational Study," *JMIR Formative Research* 5, no. 5 (May 11, 2021), https://doi.org/10.2196/27868.

15 Emily Durden, Maddison C. Pirner, Stephanie J. Rapoport, Andre Williams, Athena Robinson, and Valerie L. Forman-Hoffman, "Changes in stress, burnout, and resilience associated with an 8-week intervention with relational agent 'Woebot,'" *Internet Interventions* 33 (September 2023): 100637, https://doi.org/10.1016/j.invent.2023.100637.

16 "Sir John Kirwan's New Gig: From Coaching Rugby to How to Catch Zzzzs." *NZ Herald*, September 30, 2022.

17 Edjlali, Mo. "Digital Deepak: A Byte of Enlightenment?" *Mindful Leader*, April 18, 2023. https://www.mindfulleader.org/blog/84984-digital-deepak-a-byte-of-enlightenment.

18 Pockross, Adam. "Digital Albert Einstein Artificial Intelligence Is Here to Help with Your Science Homework." *SYFY*, November 29, 2023. https://www.syfy.com/syfy-wire/digital-albert-einstein-artificial-intelligence.

19 O'Brien, Jack. "First Look: Meet Atlantis Health's 'Digital Human.'" *MM+M - Medical Marketing and Media*, December 30, 2024. https://www.mmm-online.com/home/channel/first-look-meet-atlantis-healths-digital-human/.

20 Elliot G. Mitchell, Rosa Maimone, Andrea Cassells, Jonathan N. Tobin, Patricia Davidson, Arlene M. Smaldone, and Lena Mamykina, "Automated vs. Human Health Coaching: Exploring Participant and Practitioner Experiences," *Proceedings of the ACM on Human-Computer Interaction* 5, no. CSCW1 (April 13, 2021): 1–37, https://doi.org/10.1145/3449173.

21 Cooper, Anderson, et al. "Sal Khan Wants an AI Tutor for Every Student: Here's How It's Working at an Indiana High School." *CBS News*. December 8, 2024. https://www.cbsnews.com/news/how-khanmigo-works-in-school-classrooms-60-minutes/.

Chapter 8

1 Saxena, Asha. *The AI Factor: How to Apply Artificial Intelligence and Use Big Data to Grow Your Business Exponentially*. New York: Post Hill Press, 2023, p. 148.

2 Ilia Shumailov, Zakhar Shumaylov, Yiren Zhao, Nicolas Papernot, Ross Anderson, and Yarin Gal, "AI models collapse when trained on recursively generated data," *Nature* 631 (2024): 755–59, https://doi.org/10.1038/s41586-024-07566-y.

3 Murre, Jaap M. J., and Joeri Dros. "Replication and Analysis of Ebbinghaus' Forgetting Curve." *PLOS One*. July 6,, 2015. https://doi.org/10.1371/journal.pone.0120644.

4 David P. Ausubel and Mohamed Youssef, "The Effect of Spaced Repetition on Meaningful Retention," *The Journal of General Psychology* 73, no. 1 (1965): 147–50, https://doi.org/10.1080/00221309.1965.9711263.

5 George Vlahakis, "Meet your new AI colleague; Kelley professor studies working with digital humans," *Kelley School of Business*, published February 15, 2023, https://blog.kelley.iu.edu/2023/02/15/meet-your-new-ai-colleague-kelley-professor-studies-working-with-digital-humans/.

Chapter 9

1 Robert McCormick, "Conceptual and Procedural Knowledge," *International Journal of Technology and Design Education* 7 (January 1997): 141–59, https://doi.org/10.1023/a:1008819912213.

2 Phillip Shoemaker, "Why AI Agents Need Verified Digital Identities," *Identity*, published August 5, 2025, https://www.identity.com/why-ai-agents-need-verified-digital-identities/.

Chapter 10

1 Afraz Jaffri and Haritha Khandabattu, "Hype Cycle for Artificial Intelligence, 2024," Gartner Research, published June 17, 2024, https://www.gartner.com/en/documents/5505695.

2 "Where Do Quantum Computers Get Their Speed," *Quantum-Computing 101*, accessed May 14, 2025, http://quantumly.com/quantum-computer-speed.html.

3 Eric Mboizi, "How Is a Quantum Computer Faster than a Regular Computer?" Baeldung on Computer Science, updated March 26, 2025, https://www.baeldung.com/cs/quantum-computing-vs-regular-speed.

4 Florian Meier and Hayata Yamasaki, "Energy-Consumption Advantage of Quantum Computation," *PRX Energy* 4 (May 13, 2025): 023008, https://doi.org/10.1103/prxenergy.4.023008.

5 Press Release, "Gartner Highlights Seven Disruptions CIOs Might Not See Coming," Gartner, published September 14, 2022, https://www.gartner.com/en/newsroom/press-releases/2022-09-14-gartner-highlights-seven-disruptions-cios-might-not-s.

6 Jamie Bernardi, "Friends for sale: the rise and risks of AI companions," Ada Lovelace Institute, published January 23, 2025, https://www.adalovelaceinstitute.org/blog/ai-companions/.

7 Janna Anderson and Lee Rainie, "Being Human in 2035: How Are We Changing in the Age of AI?," Elon University's Imagining the Digital Future Center, published April 2, 2025, https://imaginingthedigitalfuture.org/wp-content/uploads/2025/03/Being-Human-in-2035-ITDF-report.pdf.

8 "Defining safe and ethical principles for Digital Humans," *Guildhawk*, published February 9, 2024, https://www.guildhawk.com/blog/defining-safe-and-ethical-principles-for-digital-humans.

9 "Our approach to ethical, responsible digital human design," *UneeQ Digital Humans*, accessed May 15, 2025, https://www.digitalhumans.com/responsible-ai.

10 Tomáš Malovec, "Navigating the Ethics of Digital Humans," *Unite.AI*, published June 17, 2024, https://www.unite.ai/navigating-the-ethics-of-digital-humans/.

Acknowledgments

Like my first book, this one benefitted enormously from input I received from my colleagues and friends. They include David Bader, Besa Bauta, Sandy Carter, Swami Chandrasekaran, Seth Dobrin, Laura Ellis, Jeff Garwood, Denisse Goldfarb, Eman Kawas, Ankur Khanna, Charlene Li, Meena Mallipeddi, Amit Prakash, and Dan Turchin. Thank you!

I also had the able assistance of many skilled people in bringing this project to completion. They include John Parsons, my editor and collaborator, Jill Marsal, my literary agent, and Caitlin Burdette and her magnificent team at Post Hill Press.

About the Author

Asha Saxena is a globally recognized technology entrepreneur, board director, Columbia University professor, and bestselling author, at the forefront of data, artificial intelligence, and digital transformation. With more than three decades of experience in technology, artificial intelligence, and business leadership, she has built and led high-impact companies, shaped executive leadership agendas, and advised global organizations on how to harness AI responsibly and strategically.

She is the founder and CEO of World Leaders in Data and AI (WLDA), a premier global leadership community advancing a fair, equitable, and innovative digital future by convening C-suite executives driving the next era of AI and data transformation. She also leads The AI Factor Institute, a strategic advisory and professional education organization that equips enterprises with the frameworks, governance structures, and capabilities needed to deploy AI at scale.

Asha is the bestselling author of *The AI Factor: How to Apply Artificial Intelligence and Use Big Data to Grow Your Business*

Exponentially, a widely adopted executive guidebook that helps leaders translate AI into measurable business outcomes. This book, *The Digital Human Advantage*, expands on her pioneering work on digital humans, enterprise productivity twins, and the future of human–AI collaboration.

At Columbia University, Asha teaches artificial intelligence and entrepreneurship at the graduate level, integrating her AI Factor methodology with real-world strategic application. She has served as Entrepreneur-in-Residence at Columbia Business School and as a partner at CEO Coaching International, guiding C-suite leaders on scaling, innovation, and value creation.

Her entrepreneurial journey includes leading successful ventures in healthcare analytics, e-commerce, and data science, including Future Technologies, a data solutions firm recognized by the World Economic Forum as a Global Growth Company. Her leadership has helped Fortune 1000 companies design resilient, high-performing, and ethical AI ecosystems.

Asha holds a BS in computer science from Bangalore University, an MS in data science from Southern Methodist University, executive education credentials from MIT and the London Business School, and a PhD in high-performance computing and artificial intelligence from the New Jersey Institute of Technology (NJIT). Her research advances digital twins cognitive augmentation and enterprise productivity models.

Through WLDA, The AI Factor Institute, and her academic work, Asha is redefining what responsible, strategic, AI leadership looks like—and empowering the next generation of innovators to build organizations that thrive in an AI-accelerated world.